Scabs Heal All Wounds

EDWARD PORCELLI

Published by Richter Publishing LLC
www.richterpublishing.com

Book Cover Design: Jessie Alarcon & Amitabha Naskar

Editors: Kati Scanlon, Monica San Nicolas, Katharina Jung & Natalie Meyer

ISBN-13: 978-1945812187

ISBN-10: 1945812184

DISCLAIMER

This book is designed to provide information on baseball only. This information is provided and sold with the knowledge that the publisher and author do not offer any legal or medical advice. In the case of a need for any such expertise consult with the appropriate professional. This book does not contain all information available on the subject. This book has not been created to be specific to any individual people or organization's situation or needs. Reasonable efforts have been made to make this book as accurate as possible. However, there may be typographical and or content errors. Therefore, this book should serve only as a general guide. This book contains information that might be dated or erroneous and is intended only to educate and entertain. The author and publisher shall have no liability or responsibility to any person or entity regarding any loss or damage incurred, or alleged to have incurred, directly or indirectly, by the information contained in this book or as a result of anyone acting or failing to act upon the information in this book. You hereby agree never to sue and to hold the author and publisher harmless from any and all claims arising out of the information contained in this book. You hereby agree to be bound by this disclaimer, covenant not to sue and release. You may return this book within the guarantee time period for a full refund. In the interest of full disclosure, this book contains affiliate links that might pay the author or publisher a commission upon any purchase from the company. While the author and publisher take no responsibility for any virus or technical issues that could be caused by such links, the business practices of these companies and or the performance of any product or service, the author or publisher has used the product or service and makes a recommendation in good faith based on that experience. All characters appearing in this work are fictitious. Any resemblance to real persons, living or dead, is purely coincidental. The opinions and stories in this book are the views of the author and not that of the publisher.

DEDICATION

From the beginning, I wanted to write this book to document the experiences I had during my playing days in the greatest game ever invented—baseball. I wanted to document them for my three daughters: Kristin, Kaitlyn, and Jennifer, so they can tell their children and future generations what their father did during one of baseball's darkest days.

This is for you...

FOREWORD

Ed Porcelli is a true example of what an individual can accomplish if he never gives up. When he first enrolled at Florida State University, there was absolutely no thought of him pitching or playing an important role in our quest to get to Omaha. As the fall progressed, he kept getting hitters out mainly by using a great sinking fastball. He never threw a pitch thinking "I hope this ball is hit at someone." He competed on every pitch!

As the spring moved into the month of March, his slider improved dramatically! We then had a reliever or spot starter that could eat up innings. You might say we trusted Ed Porcelli.

Ed's desire and determination were huge factors in Florida State Baseball playing for the National Championship in 1986.

His true character is revealed in his sincere appreciation of what others have done for him and his family. A true Seminole, he has stayed in contact with the Florida State Baseball program since his graduation.

Mike Martin

Head Coach, Florida State University Baseball

CONTENTS

ACKNOWLEDGMENTS.. i

INTRODUCTION iii

1 THE CALL 1

2 PREPARING FOR THE CHALLENGE 16

3 FIRST DAY OF SPRING TRAINING 28

4 WILTON... 39

5 UNIVERSITY OF SOUTH FLORIDA 63

6 VALIDATION 80

7 GOING FOR THE DREAM 97

8 REALIZING THE DREAM... 111

9 CONTINUING THE DREAM 127

10 FIRST WEEKS OF SPRING TRAINING 1995............................... 140

11 A FEW KIND WORDS 151

12 FIRST GAME OF SPRING... 158

13 A PLAYER'S BIGGEST FAN... 169

14 SEDONA (THE EPIPHANY) 179

15 EVERYONE HAS A NICKNAME 188

16 REALITY SETTING IN 196

17 THE FIRST DAY OF THE REST OF MY LIFE 204

18 REALITY IS STRANGER THAN... 213

EPILOGUE.. 225

REFERENCE MATERIAL... 234

ABOUT THE AUTHOR 237

ACKNOWLEDGMENTS

There are several individuals who, without their guidance, I could not have completed this over the many years it took to complete.

Brion Cummings, thank you for giving me the motivation to get this started and for sharing many of the experiences I had through my college days.

Jon Silverman, Associate Professor of English at UMass-Lowell, for his countless hours and opinions on the written words and how to convey my thoughts clearly...all without comma splices.

Florida State Head Coach Mike Martin and Tallahassee Community College Head Coach Mike McLeod—without either of you, the direction of my life would have been completely different.

Bobby Cuff and Jim Kearschner, thanks for motivating me to be the pitcher I became that could make playing professionally possible.

Steve Winterling, Lyndon Coleman, Larry Beets, and Steve Mumaw, who gave me the opportunity to coach at the college level and continue to be involved in the game I love.

Ed Durkin, for giving me the opportunity to play at the professional level and believing in me when your bosses would not.

Most of all, my wife Suzanne Goodknight...without you, none of this would be possible.

INTRODUCTION

The history of professional sports in the United States has been a tumultuous one at best. Over the past 100 years, we have seen many instances of individuals and groups associated with their respective sports cause permanent disrespect and shame. No sport has been immune to controversy, and some instances have left permanent scars.

There was the throwing of the 1919 MLB World Series that caused the ejection of eight Chicago White Sox players accused of taking bribe money to let the other team win. To this day, those individuals, including two locks to the Baseball Hall of Fame, Shoeless Joe Jackson and Eddie Cicotte, have not been reinstated by Major League Baseball (MLB). The accounts of the lasting effect of those people involved will never be forgotten and are considered one of the reasons why betting by those involved in the sport is prohibited.

The Pete Rose scandal in the late 1980s only made this problem more evident. In 1989, the future Hall of Fame player and head coach for the Cincinnati Reds was accused by the late MLB Commissioner Bart Giamatti after evidence proved that Rose bet on his team while he was coaching them. After a long court battle, Rose accepted a lifetime ban from baseball and is still not eligible for the Hall of Fame.

In 2007, the National Basketball Association (NBA) found that one of its referees had been betting on the outcome of games. After a lengthy investigation by the Federal Bureau of Investigation (FBI), it was determined that all professional and college sports can be and are currently susceptible to outside forces that "fix" the outcomes of games.

Betting on the contest by those directly involved in the outcome only proved to be the first major problem professional sports encountered in the 20th century. We have felt the effects of the racial tension of the 20th century as well. In 1947, Jackie Robinson broke the color barrier as the first African-American to play for the Brooklyn Dodgers. The ridicule and hate Robinson had to endure by not only many of his teammates, but also the opposing players, coaches, and fans, were only a fraction of what most people today know and understand.

Less than three decades later, another African-American player named Henry Aaron was about to break the all-time home run record of the sport's legendary player Babe Ruth. Early in 1974, Aaron received death threats, warning him not to continue playing and break Ruth's record. He endured and eventually retired with 755 home runs as the all-time home run leader in MLB history.

In 1968, an African-American player named Curt Flood decided to sue then MLB commissioner Bowie Kuhn and MLB on its "reserve clause" that gave the owners of major league teams the right to keep or trade players without any recourse. Flood was traded to another club and wrote a letter to Kuhn expressing his desire to be able to consider offers from other clubs before making any decisions. Kuhn denied his request and Flood sued MLB alleging that this violated anti-trust laws and the Thirteenth Amendment, which barred slavery and involuntary servitude.

The lawsuit Flood vs. Kuhn was eventually decided by the Supreme Court in 1972 with a vote of 5-3 against Flood. Although Flood lost the lawsuit, this decision paved the way toward what we know today as Free Agency. In 1973, MLB agreed to federal arbitration of salary demands, and two years later the reserve clause was thrown out that led to the free agency of players. Flood lost his personal battle in the lawsuit but won what was considered the key component of the tremendous salaries that not only MLB players get, but other professional sports players get as well.

Since 1972, there have been eight work stoppages in MLB, and three caused the loss of games played. Free agency is always one of the key issues every year that the collective bargaining agreement comes up for renewal. Other issues that have caused work stoppages are pensions (1972), salary arbitration (1973), free agency and compensation (1976, 1980, and 1981), salary cap (1990, 1994) and revenue sharing (1994). These issues all stemmed from the reserve clause elimination and the Supreme Court's decision of Flood vs. Kuhn.

Free agency is a term used to describe a professional athlete that has satisfied his contract with the previous team he played for and is now allowed to offer his services to other clubs in the sport. There are variables within the types of "free agents" (FA) that a player can be; this is usually determined by the number of years (service) he has performed at the professional level.

MLB has free agents, unrestricted free agents (UFA), type A free agents, and type B free agents. Type A FAs are the free agents considered to be in the top 20% of their position on the playing field. Type B FAs are the players in the 20-40% range of their position. UFAs are veteran players who have no restrictions on their ability to market themselves to the highest bidding team. Other professional sports have similar designations for their players, which are also determined by the amount of time the player has played since his previous contract was signed.

Salary arbitration determines the market value of the player and the amount listed in his contract. Many times, the player and the team's general manager (GM) disagree on what the player's salary should be. Both parties meet with the arbitrator who then determines what the player's salary will be. For example, a player may feel he is worth $10 million per year, but the GM feels he is only worth $7 million. The arbitrator will side with one party and assign that amount to the contract.

Salary cap is a limit on the amount that the team will pay its players in each season. All the teams agree to the same amount. Conversely, a salary floor is the minimum that each team will pay its players in each season. Teams can go over the salary cap and pay into what is called a "luxury tax," but they cannot go below the salary floor. For teams that go over the cap and pay the luxury tax, this money is distributed by MLB into items such as player benefits and industry growth. The NBA also has a luxury tax, but the proceeds from that are given back to the other teams directly.

Revenue sharing is the term for how the teams share the revenues throughout the league. All the teams in the league contribute a certain percentage of their net local revenues and then redistribute back to all the teams. Thus, small market teams like Tampa Bay and Seattle can share in the revenue of large markets like New York and Los Angeles. MLB also has a central fund that contributes funds to each team based on their revenue streams.

The collective bargaining agreement (CBA) is the term for when the players and owners sit down and discuss how they are going to move forward and divide the income that is generated from television revenue and ticket sales through concessions and merchandise. Even video games that have the likeness of players and teams are discussed and bargained between the owners and players. When either side does not like how the revenues are being distributed, they negotiate when the contract is up for renewal. When all items up for discussion are agreed upon, the CBA is signed and the contract is generally good for five years.

Work stoppages occur when the players strike or the owners "lockout" the players from playing. This happens when one of the two sides will not relent on one or more of the topics during the negotiations. Of the eight work stoppages since 1972, three were lockouts and five were strikes.

Baseball has certainly paid the price over the years with its work stoppages, betting scandals, and court battles. It has continued to endure because of its popularity and resilience when something controversial happens. However, something about what was happening in the late '80s leading up to the strike in 1994 made it different.

There had been a growing amount of distrust between the players and owners since 1987 when the players' union won three grievances from the owners due to collusion—the clubs acted in consort to help facilitate the decrease of players' salaries by agreeing to not sign them. The players were awarded $280 million collectively for the grievances and still did not trust the owners seven years later. The next CBA that was signed in 1990 did little to help the owners control spending and large market teams would end up in bidding wars that would cause salaries to skyrocket over the next two years. From 1989 to 1992, the average salary more than doubled from $490,000 to over $1 million and there were no signs of it slowing down. The players, still remembering the owners colluding in the mid '80s, were preparing for the worst as the new CBA was to be signed by December 31, 1994.

As the negotiations started in January of 1994, the owners were determined to break the union. Making things worse for the players is that one of the owners, Bud Selig of the Milwaukee Brewers, was named as the acting commissioner of baseball due to the forced resignation of Fay Vincent. Selig and Jerry Reinsdorf, the owner of the Chicago White Sox, were the most critical of Vincent and after the repeated verbal attacks and accusations, Vincent finally relented. With Selig now acting as commissioner de facto for the owners, he would be the puppet that the owners needed to get their demands met in the next CBA.

In June of 1994, the owners presented their new CBA for the players to consider that had taken out much of what the players had bargained for over the past 20 years. A salary cap was initiated, salary arbitration was eliminated, and free agency would be limited to players with four years of service. The players' representative, an attorney named Donald Fehr, summed it up after reading the owners' proposal:

"They eliminate salary arbitration, add a cap, and pose all sorts of limitations on free agency. Put all those things together, and you've cut the heart out of the player compensation system."

The owners knew the players would never sign a deal giving up so much. It was a slap in the face to the players, and they knew right then that there would certainly be a strike.

Then in July, the owners failed to make a nearly $8 million payment to the players for their proceeds of the All-Star game and then suspended the payments to the players' pension fund. It was all but over; on July 28, the players voted to strike on August 12th and the fight between the owners and players begun.

The talk of using replacement players did not start heating up until after Selig officially canceled the World Series on September 14th. It was just a myth. In fact, nobody really believed that it could possibly happen. Two months passed and nothing was accomplished on the negotiating table. Then on December 6, Richard Ravitch stepped down as the chief negotiator for the owners. Soon after, the owners voted on a salary cap that was accepted and implemented on December 23—without the approval of the Players' Association.

When the owners voted on the salary cap and unilaterally changed the bargaining agreement, it infuriated the players' union. The impasse between the two groups were further apart than ever. On January 5, Donald Fehr declared all 895 unsigned players as free agents in response to the owners making unilateral changes to the CBA, and the arbitrator agreed. Eleven players were awarded nearly $10 million because of the collusion by the owners and on February 1st, they scrapped the cap and went back to the old agreement.

I remember in early December calling Ed Durkin, who was a scout with the Milwaukee Brewers at the time. He had coached an amateur team I had played for a few years earlier, and I wanted to get his angle on what was going on. I also wanted to know if they were going to consider bringing in replacement players should an agreement not be made. He said the organization (and the other clubs as well) had "earmarked" players for the start of the season should they not have a CBA in place. Three weeks later, just after Christmas, Durkin called me with the news that not only was the MLB Players Association on strike, but their minor-league players were not going to play either. This was really when it started to sink in that we might get the chance to play.

Finally, on January 26 at Valencia Community College in Orlando, the Brewers held a tryout specifically for players to be used as replacements—scabs.

What is a "Scab"?

Dictionary.com has provided us with several different definitions. We will get familiar with one of the lesser used definitions...

SCAB (noun)

1. the incrustation that forms over a sore or wound during healing.

2. Veterinary Pathology. a mangy disease in animals, especially sheep; scabies.

3. Plant Pathology. a disease of plants characterized by crustlike lesions on the affected parts and caused by a fungus or bacterium. One of these crust like lesions.

4. a worker who refuses to join a labor union or to participate in a union strike, who takes a striking worker's place on the job, or the like.

5. Slang. a rascal or scoundrel.

6. Metallurgy. a projection or roughness on an ingot or casting from a defective mold. A surface defect on an iron or steel piece resulting from the rolling in of scale.

7. Carpentry. A short, flat piece of wood used for various purposes, as binding two timbers butted together or strengthening a timber at a weak spot.

verb (used without object), scabbed, scabbing.

8. to become covered with a scab.

9. to act or work as a scab.

Many of those players on the field that day were not thinking about the ramifications of what laid before them should they get signed that day. For me, it was just the belief that I could compete with others at the highest level possible.

Competition is always key; we only cared about the competition. What we didn't expect was how much reaction the replacement players would get from the media, fans, coaches, the Major League Baseball Players Association (MLBPA), and the rest of the other players just trying to compete.

1 THE CALL

January 1995

It was a Thursday evening when I received the call that I had waited for all my life...

"Hello?" I said.

"Hey, Eddie. Ed Durkin here. How are ya?"

"Fine, Ed. What's up?"

"Hey, Eddie—how would you like to be a Brewer?"

"Durk, how did you do it? I thought I wasn't gonna be able to get on..."

"Well, we had a couple of guys who went with the Yanks. It left a few spots open, so I got in your corner and sold it to Fred Stanley. Don't let me down, Eddie! You're going to Chandler!"

The next day, we met at a Boston Market and he produced a professional baseball contract with the Milwaukee Brewers. Another one of my dreams had come to fruition. It was a surreal experience, to say the least, and unfortunately not a lottery ticket either. It's not often that a 29-year-old guy signs his first professional contract. Most likely, a situation in which that happens is an unusual one. Most professional baseball players my age are either in the major leagues or out of baseball! I'd tried to get signed in previous years, but I gave up after turning 22.

Running my wife's family business in Clearwater certainly didn't match up with any aspect of playing professional baseball, especially in the retail industry. However, I'd learned the business, was particularly fond of working directly with clients and knew how to deliver. Dry cleaning really isn't what 10-year-old kids dream of doing—fantasizing about getting the mustard stain out of your khakis—if you know what I mean. Here was the chance to get out of Dodge (even if it was only for a few weeks) and go to a real life "fantasy camp" that you don't have to pay for—they pay you! It was a chance to play this game as a professional, in a class above amateur status, and play with, and against, the best players in the world.

Looking back and remembering the situation that led up to the improbable MLB labor strike, it was just a few short weeks since talking with Ed Durkin until we'd have this chance. It was less than a week removed that we had the tryout at Valencia Community College in Orlando. Over 120 prospective players came to be signed in the aftermath of a pivotal time in baseball history. I originally spoke with Durkin when they started to talk about using replacement players in MLB in late December because the labor negotiation talks were going nowhere. Eddie said they had "earmarked" players and pitchers in the organization that would carry out that task should it come down to that. Just one week later, he called back. Only three players in the entire organization agreed to play in "scab" exhibition games. Milwaukee would hold a tryout in Orlando that would be open to only those players that had formal professional experience.

The owners of the teams had made it clear that making a mockery of the game would serve no purpose. This would only alienate the fans that were actually against the players' union.

Knowing that I had no experience, Durk said, "Don't worry about it. I have already cleared your participation with the organization. That doesn't mean you'll make the squad or get signed, but you'll get to tryout."

A few other players I knew would also be invited—fellow teammate Bobby Cuff and recently released Stacy Burdick among them. Bobby played on the same amateur baseball team as me, the St. Pete Hurricanes, and we knew Stacy from summer ball in college. After posting an 11-4 record for the MLB Baltimore Orioles AA minor league team, Stacy developed an arm injury after that season and was subsequently released in 1991.

Like most other kids growing up, baseball had been a huge part of our lives, whether it was playing, watching, or coaching. For most, that involvement ends by the time we're 17 and is rekindled again with our own children.

We just never had the desire to grow up, so to speak, and we played through college—and for Bobby, it was getting drafted by the Blue Jays in 1988. Even after his short stint getting released less than a year after getting signed, he got involved with the Hurricanes and has been there ever since.

The Hurricanes are a local amateur league team that plays in Pinellas County, Florida and was nothing other than legendary during the mid to late '90s. The team won multiple national tournaments and was still made up of primarily ex-Division I college and ex-professional players. Over the years, the

3

Hurricanes have endured the changeover as most MLB clubs to compete with other 18+ teams. This team still exists today, and many of the players who played in the '90s are still competing against 18-year-olds.

Amateur baseball leagues have many different divisions that combine age requirements, and some are wood bat leagues as opposed to metal. These leagues are all over the country and regulated by the Men's Senior Baseball League (MSBL) and Men's Amateur Baseball League (MSBL). They have given those who were not skilled or fortunate enough to play pro ball a chance to continue to play the game they love.

To be ready for the tryout in Orlando, we decided to schedule a few games with some teams in our league to keep us in playing shape. There is no substitute for live pitching, and only regular games could provide this. Although we believed it would never come down to the tryout being held, we took the possibility of it very seriously. I mean, it was hard to believe MLB could actually have replacement players starting for spring training.

Remember how the NFL had replacement players in 1981? The backlash from it was astounding, and both the fans and the media said it made a mockery of the game and cheapened it. It was as if these "players" on the field were incapable of performing. The fact was, the unfamiliarity of these replacements had more to do with it than their performance did. The players that the NFL put out during the strike were good players and many played in major Division I programs. Most of the average fans didn't know them, so they naturally believed they were incapable of playing at a higher level.

Many fans couldn't even tell the difference between a highly skilled offensive lineman and an average one. How they move their feet and use their hands. How they react to counter moves by their corresponding defensive lineman and prevent the player from tackling the quarterback. Yet fans were some of the biggest critics of how the replacements could not put out an entertaining product.

Another issue that you must consider is the media coverage of a strike. The minute there happens to be some blunder on the field, the media will be quick to judge, as if the replacements don't know what they're doing and aren't qualified to be out there. This country has seen replacements due to strikes during many of the labor crises of major professional sports over the past decades.

In 2013, the NFL had the strike involving the referees' union. Day after day went by while the media destroyed these men who were reffing these games to the best of their ability. The media pointed out every bad call they made. The media did not have one positive comment regarding these refs during the entire time they were involved. Granted, some were not ready for the speed involved in the early games, but many improved drastically after adjusting themselves to the quickness of the players. Still, both the fans and the media were enthusiastic about the eventual end of the strike and the return of the seasoned referees.

When Bobby and I were preparing for the tryout, we never thought about the repercussions caused by the labor dispute. We didn't think about taking jobs from players who had played baseball at the highest level. The history of previous labor strikes and lockouts never entered our minds or the fallout of the collateral damage left in the aftermath. Our only thoughts were to put on an MLB jersey and compete on the biggest stage in the world.

We knew that putting on the Brewers uniform would create dissension with many fans and media members, just not how much. We just wanted to play the game at its highest level and compete.

As December approached, the players' union and the owners were growing further apart. The reports tried to give a glimmer of hope that the players would concede, but at every meeting they had, one side would eventually walk out on the other. Most everybody wanted this to be over by now with the exception of the replacement players on the verge of signing contracts. Every evening the lead story would be an update on the strike and how the impasse was inevitable. Not only did we start believing that there was a chance to get signed and to play during the exhibition season, but we also believed that we might play in some regular season games. Spring training was only 60 days away, and the experts said that it would take significant concessions on both sides to come to an agreement before then.

This news fueled our fire, and we were as ready for the tryout as we could ever be. Each day had a purpose. We spent our mornings and afternoons working the day job, and for our evenings, we'd train. Our minds were filled with promise that gave us the drive to work harder than ever before. The culmination was to say we were involved in one of the most controversial times in the history of baseball.

The last few days before the tryout at Valencia Community College were probably the easiest. During the weeks leading up to the tryouts, we fully expected the players and owners to come to an agreement. The feelings of anticipation and anxiousness became an everyday love affair that we simply couldn't walk away from. We couldn't concentrate on our jobs anymore, only think and dream about what was in front of us if this escalated into regular season games. It was still too far out of reach, but we could taste it.

Now that it had become a realization that the replacement players would be invited to spring training, the anxiety turned to focus. You get one shot to impress the scouts and coaches enough to be offered a contract, so you better make it count! The last week, we prepared diligently and with purpose.

The tryout was on a Wednesday morning, so our last throwing day would be Monday. Remembering that day with Bobby down at the Payson complex in St. Petersburg, our workouts were flawless in executing our pitches. We were in the best shape of our pitching lives—probably caused by the adrenaline created by the situation. We really had no idea of how the event would be held or how many pitches we would throw. Would we throw in the bullpen or against live hitters in game situations? We had to be ready for everything. We talked about each scenario and the strategies to overcome them. In the end, we agreed to just do one thing: get rest and be ready to have the best day of our lives. Next stop, Orlando!

Wednesday morning was clear and cold. We were to report at 9 a.m. for an informational session before they would start. Ed Durkin was a regional scout at the time and responsible for many of the players and pitchers that were there that morning. Central Florida was in his backyard.

Ed had been with Milwaukee since the late 1980s when he'd provided the club (for free) his choices in each round of the MLB amateur draft. After it was apparent that his picks were accurately reflected in the draft, they decided to offer him a position as a scout. He signed some important players for Milwaukee, most notably Gary Sheffield. The head of the Milwaukee scouting department, Ken Califano, would be running the tryout while various other scouts would be there to observe. There must have been over 120 players there for them to look at, about 40 to 45 of them being pitchers.

The time was approaching for the tryout to commence, and Califano addressed the players. Shortly through his welcome of the players to the tryout that morning, he quickly made it a point to remind all those who were about to hit the field.

"Only those players who have documented experience as former professional players will be considered. If you do not meet this criteria, you will not be signed and will be asked to leave the field immediately," he said with authority.

I felt the hair go up on the back of my neck and all the blood exited my head with great despair. Ed had said that he'd already spoken with the staff about my situation. What if he was mistaken? The meeting ended after 20 minutes, telling us how they were going to conduct the tryout and breaking us down into more manageable groups. After he was finished, Durkin started talking to me before the words came out.

"Eddie, don't worry, you're cool. Just go out there and pitch your ass off when it's your turn."

This was good enough for me.

There were many other teams holding their own tryouts all over Florida, Arizona, and California during this month. Some of the guys at our camp were talking about the other camps they would attend to get a shot. The Yankees, Blue Jays, and Mets were all holding their tryouts this week as well, but getting invited to them was unlikely. This invite was through my relationship with Ed, so I had to make the most of it. There'd be no other opportunities.

I met Ed after moving back from Cleveland, Ohio in 1987. I hadn't gotten drafted after the 1987 season and a change of scenery sounded like what the doctor ordered. Fresh out of college, looking for a career was about as foreign as anything I'd ever encountered. Jobs were not easy to come by unless you were into selling insurance to all your friends and family. There were baseball leagues to play in and it wouldn't take long before finding both an apartment and job, so I started looking for a team to play on for the rest of the summer. Through a mutual friend, I was introduced to Durkin and started playing for his team in Clearwater.

With my background, Ed immediately began me as a starting pitcher as well as a reliever in some of the tournaments that summer. One tournament in Ft. Myers, I made five appearances in four days, which Ed still talks about to this day. He'd remark that if he did that now, he'd be accused of overthrowing me and jeopardizing my arm.

"He kept on saying 'give me the ball', so I gave it to him." Ed would laugh as he remembered.

Later that summer, we had a tournament in Jacksonville where we faced the Suns. There were a couple of ex-teammates on that team from FSU—Mike Holman and BJ Guzzone. That day was my best performance of the season, throwing nine innings and giving up only three hits. I struck out 12. After the game, Durkin came to me and asked about playing professional ball. Still not aware he was a scout with the Brewers, my response was not what he was looking for. I gave Ed a half-hearted answer that I really didn't care about pro baseball, I was just enjoying my time playing when I could.

It was "the fork in the road of life" that we are unaware of, not understanding that you're in a decision moment that will forever change your life. Looking back, I wonder what would've been. Baseball is a funny game when you boil it down because it mimics life and how the impossible becomes possible. The possibilities are endless of how it might have turned out.

Being a little older (21 at the time), I knew how to pitch and set up hitters. Players like that go unnoticed because they're not flashy, lighting up the radar gun. Pitchers with great stuff learn how to pitch after many years in the majors only because they lose the velocity they had in earlier years. Playing professional baseball was a lifelong dream and if given the chance, it should've been taken. I would've been on a plane to Helena, Montana, that week and a dream would have been a reality. With hard work and a little luck, it was possible to move up in an organization. Baseball is as political as any other business, but if a pitcher could get hitters out, there was a place for them. The hardest part for pitchers like that was to get signed, but it became easier once they were in the organization.

So, as the morning wore on during the tryout, it was apparent that most of the time, the pitchers sat around waiting for their turn to prove their worth. The ABC late night show *Nightline* was there, as the reality of the eminent baseball strike was becoming a major news story throughout the country.

It was obvious that some of the players there were grossly out of shape and overmatched by their pitching counterparts. There was a long batting practice before live game situations so the coaches and scouts could look at what they had to deal with for the morning. *Nightline* was filming and interviewing the scouts and coaches on what they were seeing with these possible replacements. They weren't impressed. Durkin was being interviewed by the commentator as one of the hitters was taking batting practice and was overmatched by the coach pitching. After about 45 seconds of watching this "player" miss 10 consecutive pitches (and looked very bad doing so), Durkin commented to the interviewer, "This guy is just going to need to find another vocation in life."

Believe it or not, that quote made it on that night's broadcast of *Nightline*.

As batting practice ended, the pitchers started to get themselves loose, knowing that it was their turn to impress. There was no bullpen session—the term used for pitchers to work with coaches on the mechanics, pitches, etc. We were to get three or four hitters, and that would be our tryout. It was going to be a while if we were among the last guys to throw. Sitting and waiting was the hardest part because adrenaline was pumping and we wanted to pitch, but we had to back off or we'd spend it on the sidelines!

It'd be over an hour before it was my turn, so I had to just relax. I watched the other pitchers and saw what I was up against. The pitchers in this tryout were certainly in better shape than their player counterparts. Not only were they in shape, but they looked well-polished and in mid-season form. This is usually the case when it comes to spring training—pitchers and catchers are usually in a week before the rest of the players.

Spring training had changed dramatically over the past 80 years in both football and baseball. It used to be that preseason was to get into shape to be ready to go. What most people are unaware of is that these players usually had second and third jobs to pay the bills because their "hobby" didn't. As the professional leagues grew, players started to demand more of a cut of the profits and deservedly so. These players were in a much better position to not need the extra jobs. Then back in the late '60s, a man by the name of Curt Flood changed the entire dynamics of professional sports through the inception of free agency.

Free agency allowed players to offer their services to other clubs and could choose their place of work. Before 1969, MLB had what was known as the "reserve clause." This stated that a player's rights are retained by the team he plays for after the expiration of his contract, regardless of whether he performed to the expectations of the contract.

The time to pitch was quickly approaching and the need to be at the top of my game was essential. Bobby was finished with his tryout and was relieved. He had pitched well with good velocity and control, but most importantly his out pitch, the splitter, was well above average. Like always, he talked about all the mistakes he made instead of the good pitches, but was pleased with the outing. The time for me to pitch was quickly approaching and the need to be at the top of my game was essential. So, as I was heating up he was throttling down, roles became reversed, and the anxiety started to set in.

Leaving the bullpen mound was exhilarating. During the warmup pitches, I kept telling myself—*just do something that makes those scouts think I'm different*. Finally, I finished the last warmup pitch and the first batter stepped into the batter's box.

A feeling of euphoria came over me, and I did not hear a sound. That is one of the most interesting things about pitching. You become extremely focused on the task at hand and everything around you disappears. This is depicted well in Kevin Costner's movie *For Love of the Game* when he starts each inning saying to himself, "activate the mechanism." I looked to the catcher as he squatted down and put his right hand down with one index finger extended to throw a fastball. With a steady deep breath, I exhaled and started my tryout.

With the second pitch I threw, the first batter bled a hit between the third baseman and shortstop. I thought to myself, *Great...so much for not letting somebody on*.

It wasn't hit that great and these fielders weren't the best, either, so I told myself, *let's just induce a ground ball for two here*. Three pitches later, that's exactly what occurred after the batter hit a slider to the shortstop. However, the ball wasn't hit very hard and the batter beat the throw from second, so only one out was made. The next batter hit a one-two outside fastball lazily into right for the second out. The fastball was a good pitch with a velocity in the mid-80s, and had nice movement from left to right, but again nothing that'd be considered different from the others. The third batter hit an easy ground ball to the second baseman and ended the inning, but as my turn was over, the coaches told me to stay out on the mound for the next hitter.

It was great to have the extra work, and at least it seemed that I was making progress with the coaches and might be considered for a roster spot. The next hitter got on base due to a throwing error when I was told that the next hitter would be the last. Even though I had an opportunity to show all the pitches I was capable of throwing, it still felt like I needed something more. After running the count to 3-2, I decided to throw the slider instead of the fastball. Sometimes it's necessary to show confidence in throwing certain pitches, regardless of the situation. I figured by throwing it properly, the batter would freeze and leave the bat on his shoulder, which is exactly what happened. The pitch was perfectly executed and bisected the plate for a called third strike. My mission of standing out from the other pitchers was accomplished.

Now that I was done pitching, I had to wait for the rest of the players and pitchers to finish up. You could tell the tryout was winding down as many players were talking, goofing around, and packing up their stuff. The very fact that you could hear voices other than those of the people running the event was evidence enough. Most were nervous and not talking in the beginning of the tryout, focusing on the task at hand. Finally, Califano gathered up the players and thanked them for participating. Someone from the organization would contact them if they would be considered as a replacement player.

There were some pitchers told to stay after the event was over. Bobby was one, as well as Stacy Burdick, Scott Diaz, Dave Reichle, and three others. They were all signed to minor league contracts and were on their way to Chandler in February.

Feeling a bit depressed for not being chosen, I was still elated for Bobby. He'd worked very hard and certainly deserved it. He was worried about his elbow—being 29 meant you weren't the youngest in the crowd and having a hurt arm wouldn't help his chances in the long run. Bobby felt bad for me and almost felt guilty for the way the tryout had unfolded. We talked about how some of the other teams were holding tryouts in a similar fashion and that there was still hope. We knew Durkin was my only chance because he knew my ability and could make the roster despite having no pro experience. Bob and I talked about the chances of getting signed by another club before replacement players would report to camp, but we both knew my best chance was with Durkin. Still, I was happy for Bobby and celebrated his signing and the excitement of his opportunity.

Later that evening, Durkin called and said he was pulling for me, but the decision ultimately came from Califano. He was positive about the performance that day and told me not to give up hope to hook up with some other club. Eddie said he'd put in a good word for the next tryout as many of the scouts for the other teams knew him well, and we left it at that. It started to set in that this wasn't going to be the opportunity to pitch for Milwaukee, or most likely any other team. Then feelings of despair, frustration, and realization set in as I drove back home and thought about the lost opportunity.

The evenings while lying in bed were when it was the worst; I did nothing but think about how I could've performed better to change their minds. It was clearly the best chance I'd had to sign a professional contract in the past four years and the hard work, preparation, and dedication over the past two months felt wasted. I thought I had done the job well enough to be considered, but no, there was nothing left to do now but watch Bobby be a part of MLB history.

The next day was sports trivia night with the guys, and with the tryout the day before, we had plenty of reasons to celebrate. Bobby was going to Arizona and we were all excited for him. All the pitchers on our team—Jim Kearcshner, Danny Tunnell, and myself plus a few others—were very supportive of his success.

Jim had tried out with the Blue Jays that week and was not selected either, so we had something in common. We threw about the same, so we figured again that it must be the velocity that held us back. Bobby was consistently in the upper 80s, so he had no issues with that. Still, there was a feeling of loss that didn't seem to subside, like that dull headache that just won't go away. It'd be exciting to hear about the preseason from Bob's perspective as a player on the front line, so this wasn't a total loss for me.

Durkin then called me with the good news that I'd be making the trip as well. I felt the hair raise up on the back of my neck now knowing that I would be joining Bobby in Arizona. To be given the chance to compete was overwhelming, and I felt the blood in my veins start to circulate—my heart was starting to pound and I needed to calm myself down before I risked hyperventilating! The resurgence of life was exhilarating and I knew that if given the chance, I could make the team and maybe even pitch on the greatest stage in the world.

Those six days before Eddie Durkin called me were some of the darkest in my life, but Durkin made it happen. I would be on that plane to experience this once-in-a-lifetime event of epic proportions. They canceled the World Series...the World Series, for crying out loud! If the owners of MLB were going to put up with canceling the World Series, who knew what would happen next. This baseball strike was going to be one wild ride, and I would have a front seat for it!

2 PREPARING FOR THE CHALLENGE

Naturally, we were glued to ESPN and other news sources every day to catch any news regarding the strike. Bobby and I were obviously excited for the challenge that would start on February 12th. We were still a long way off from the day we'd board the plane to Arizona.

News sources throughout the country were reporting about the tryouts for replacement players. There was no progress being made in the labor negotiations and the teams were preparing for a spring training with scabs. The media was saying that both sides should lock themselves in a room and order in food until they came to an agreement. This viewpoint didn't make any sense. The owners had nothing to lose at this point; they had already canceled the World Series and were all in. The pompous attitude of the players—a byproduct of the most powerful labor union in U.S. history—let them assume that eventually the owners would cave.

This wasn't a game of chicken between two cars on Hwy. 9. This was two jumbo jet airliners flying toward a head-on collision course at 35,000 feet! The damage would be irreparable if the season started with the replacements. Although Bob and I would certainly enjoy this, we also knew it would damage the game.

In an interview with Charlie Rose in September, Bob Costas said the sides were so far apart, they should get all their issues repaired and start the season on August 11, 1995, a year from the day the players walked off the job. They would pick up all their statistics where they were left off and finish the season. It would be called the 1994-1995 season. This wasn't a bad idea from one of the most intelligent analysts and announcers in MLB. Many believe his ideas were progressive enough to consider him as the MLB Commissioner.

Most critics to this day believe Selig has been one of the worst commissioners in baseball history, and for the most part, they're correct. There has been much controversy surrounding Selig because he was put into the position by the owners to rubber stamp the agenda they desired. The problem with Costas's opinion was that the owners wouldn't be able to just do what they wanted "for the best interests of baseball." For the past 25 years, I'd thought of the phrase "for the best interests of the owners" when Selig said that. I'd always understood the players when it came to the distrust they had in regards to the owners.

Of course, there was a lot more involved with this impasse than what was on the surface. The vast majority of the public really had no idea of the detailed issues facing the owners and players. It was a time where the news coverage every day comprised of interviewing player representatives, the owners' representative, and what was accomplished during that day's meeting.

From mid-January all the way up to the beginning of camp, it was like Groundhog Day all over again. It was the same interviews and the same answers by the same people every night. Even President Clinton tried to get involved by imposing a February 5th deadline for an agreement that didn't result in the sides coming together. That was just 10 days away from when Bobby and I were to report in Chandler, and that was the day we knew that we'd be going to Arizona. If the president couldn't get them to come to an agreement, nothing was going to prevent it from happening.

The 10 days or so before we were to report were the days for us to get in as good of shape as possible. The first thing the clubs did when you got to camp was give players a physical, so passing that was imperative. It'd be an embarrassing tragedy to go through all of this just to get onto a plane after failing the physical. Oh, and yes—you had to buy the ticket home! Really, the getting in shape for us was the long distance running that most pitchers had to do during the spring. We'd both had to do that in college and detested running in general, but you had to be able to do this without looking like you hadn't run in 10 years. Due to what was at stake, we had little need for the motivation and built up enough endurance before we left so it wouldn't be an issue.

As for being ready to pitch, Bobby and I were in as good of shape as possible. We had pitched in scrimmages leading up to spring training, and we were ready to play. The hardest part was concentrating on our jobs and securing them before we left. Since I worked in the family business, my situation was set. However, Bobby had only worked at the VA hospital in Largo for a few years without any assurances of his job being there when he got back. Like most employers, they knew the situation going on in MLB, and many who had an employee signed to play in the strike thought it was cool. Some employers were adamant in regard to those who left that their job may not be there when they returned. Some players left their jobs with no assurance that the strike would last more than a couple of days after the replacements reported to camp. Perhaps those who made this risk came back more marketable with an experience they'd tell people for a lifetime.

Working during those two to three weeks before camp for me was difficult because my mind was constantly thinking about how it was going to be in Arizona. Something would always trigger the thought of starting baseball and getting ready for the trip, like that feeling when you wait all year long for summer vacation; sometimes the anticipation of the time approaching felt more fun than the trip itself. This was not fun, only tortuous! There were times we thought that the day would never come, or even worse, that the strike would get settled. Those anxious days leading up to the week we were to report were absolutely the worst.

On January 26th, the same day as the tryout, President Clinton ordered both sides to go back to the bargaining table and have an agreement by February 5th. The government had gotten involved in early January by introducing bills into Congress specifically to end the strike. In response, Donald Fehr, the executive director of the MLBPA, declared all 895 unsigned players as free agents because of the unilateral changes in contracts of MLB players by the owners, and an arbitrator awarded $10 million to 11 players that were affected by this change.

Back then, none of us were thinking about what would be 20 years down the line as we boarded the planes to Phoenix. Just the day before, I'd said my goodbyes to my family and co-workers at the cleaners then went to dinner with my wife.

We talked about what the next couple of months would be like with me being away. It was going to be a difficult time for us financially; we'd just bought a new house in Clearwater, and although the money I made at the cleaners wasn't much, it still helped to pay the mortgage. I was a bit surprised that my in-laws didn't help us more during this unusual period. I had decided to dedicate myself to a career in the family business to help it grow and eventually own it one day with my wife. I worked well over 60 hours a week and made it clear to her family that I was taking less money as a "commitment" to the family business. I was too forgiving a person to see that it was all a façade. The experience during this time would certainly be a determining factor of the course of events after the strike ended.

The players would be paid for the time we were in Chandler, and I'd be sending money back home at every chance, but it was an unknown factor for us at the time.

We didn't live extravagantly. We lived modestly and saved for retirement. We even purchased some stock for the first time that year. It was an unsettling time in our lives; I had sacrificed my degree for the chance to help build my wife's family business, believing that someday we'd own the chain of cleaning stores. It became one of the reasons we ended up divorced. It was another one of those decisions you make without the ability to see into a crystal ball to know where it would lead. With that, Lisa and I made our final arrangements that evening, and I packed to get on the next morning's flight to Arizona.

That first day was filled with both excitement and anxiety. The unknown factor of what would happen in the coming weeks was enough to raise my blood pressure. Just trying to chill out was impossible; then again, I'd always been a bit excitable in the first place. My exuberance had always shown on the baseball field, but this was a bit over the top. I wasn't one who generally talked to people while on a plane. I preferred to keep to myself and let people enjoy their peace, but occasionally I would talk when the person next to me spoke first.

Looking at the itinerary of the next few days, the gentleman sitting next to me noticed I was involved with baseball in some capacity. He introduced himself and (like everybody else) seemed to have an opinion about the labor dispute. He didn't like the idea of "replacement" guys trying to break the union, but understood why we'd take this opportunity to play. I explained that for many of these players, this was their only chance to get looked at by the upper management of their respective teams.

Continuing my conversation with the gentleman on the plane, I spoke with him about my own close calls in getting signed over the past five years. He understood the position many of us were in. As we landed in St. Louis for the layover, I thanked him for his questions, and he wished me luck over the coming months. However, he still hoped they'd start opening day on time with the striking players.

I kept to myself on the next flight, still stinging a bit from my conversation with the passenger on the previous flight. It made me wonder how the replacement players would be received once the games started should the strike get that far.

My conversation with the guy from St. Louis had made it clear that very few people could possibly empathize with the players. How many people played baseball after Little League, anyway? The actual idea of playing would be foreign to most fans of the game. They grew up watching players break into the majors and retire, too. Their only continuity was the players—the names and numbers and team they play for. Nothing else. To completely change over to an entire roster of unknowns would be the real challenge that faced us ahead. Could you get a fanbase to get behind a bunch of players they've never seen on the field and watch them play against a bunch more?

As we had started our descent, I looked out the window and was embraced by scenes of desert and cactus plants. Thirty minutes later, we had landed and my life in professional baseball was about to start.

It didn't take long for a representative to take us to our new home for the indefinite future—The Quality Inn in Phoenix at the intersection of I-10 and Elliot Rd, affectionately known as "Dobson Ranch." I was hoping to room with Bobby, but instead I met Brian Tollberg, my roomie for the spring. When everybody had finally arrived, it was clear they roomed all the players that were signed as replacements together.

At first, we thought this would be a dead giveaway and that we'd be looked at by the other players in camp differently. We didn't want the others to know for obvious reasons, but this rooming situation wouldn't help us blend in with the crowd at chowtime. It was early afternoon, and there was really nothing to do except get acquainted with our surroundings. Bob and I decided to cross the bridge over I-10 (which became our daily routine after practice) and check out civilization.

Neither of us had the money to rent a car, and transportation was to be provided throughout our time in Chandler. It was about 15 minutes to the spring training facility by bus and a brutally long walk, so you didn't want to miss it on the way back. It was clear that most of the time we'd be at the training site and here, at the closest shopping center near the hotel. For the time being, this suited us fine. We were both financially strapped and would be sending money back to Florida except for what was needed for our evening meals.

Knowing they'd be feeding us at the complex for lunch, we were hoping to occasionally sneak out sandwiches to save money—a common practice for any college athlete. Every evening after a game at Florida State, we'd try to be the first guy to the concession stand in the stadium to ransack whatever didn't get sold. Every dollar that didn't get spent on food could go to a more practical purchase—draft beer! That'd have to wait in this case, as we wanted to make an impression. We knew what camp was going to be like so we got back to the hotel early. We were tired from the time change and needed to get ready for our physicals in the morning.

Morning breakfast was between 7 and 7:45 a.m. It was considered a mandatory activity. Any mandatory activity that a player missed was subject to a $50 fine, and the money was the least of your worries should it happen. We were already on thin ice as it was and didn't want to be noticed anywhere but on a ball field, which made this no issue for us.

It wouldn't take long to notice who the non-replacements were. We had recognized a few from college—Jeff D'Amico from Northeast High in St. Petersburg was one, and Mark Loretta another. Some other notables were Anthony Williamson, 4th pick overall in 1994, and Joe Wagner, 39th pick. Bob and I knew they wouldn't be playing in anything other than scrimmage games before the exhibition season started.

Most of the players minded their own business. They sat together in cliques, and we sat alone on the other side of the hotel conference room. Being new to the organization, the best thing we could do was keep our heads down and mind our own business. Until you got the chance to get to know things and how things worked on *this* team, it was best to keep a low profile. Not that turnover was foreign to most of these guys. Every spring brought a new bunch of guys from the winter transactions with other clubs. Unless you were paying attention each day, you didn't really know where they came from. We were clearly older than most (if not all) the players eating breakfast that morning. We were sure as the eyes ran across the room that many suspected why we were there.

We finished, went back to the room, and awaited our assigned time to head to the facility for our physicals. There were over eighty players in camp and they were sending us to the facility around 20 at a time. Once there, most of the players were in good spirits. They joked around most of the time and talked about the labor dispute in general. One player waiting, Tim Dell, made no bones about his participation and willingness to sign to play in the replacement games.

Tim was drafted in the 28th round by the Philadelphia Phillies in 1988, and was dealt to the Brewers in 1991. After a good year in Stockton, California, for the Class A+ Stockton Ports in 1991, he was promoted to the Class AA El Paso Diablos in 1992. Dell struggled to keep his ERA below five, and Milwaukee had apparently approached Dell in the off-season to participate in spring training.

They told Tim that his days as a Brewer were numbered. I believe that Tim just thought he might as well get paid before getting released. Dell thought, "I'm twenty-six and probably won't get picked up after the spring, anyway." Waiting for our turn to get our physical and listening to Dell was hysterical. The one thing about these baseball players was that they usually had a great sense of humor and were very self-deprecating—as was the case with Tim. Another player waiting in line was Robert Kappesser.

Bob "Kappy" Kappesser was an undrafted career minor league catcher that was signed by Milwaukee in 1989. Kappy had a great view on life, and it was apparent that he too had enough of the politics in baseball. He also would eventually be among the existing players in the organization crossing the line.

He was always smiling, quick-witted, and honest. He could be relentless if he saw weakness in another player. He gained the moniker "Kappy" for his bald head and constantly wearing a catcher's shell whether he was in the game or not.

Kappy was an easy guy to like. He was one of those guys who always kept the dugout loose with his humor and quick wit. *It's going to be an interesting spring!* I thought.

After watching Dell and Kappesser clown around for a while, the turn to get my physical finally came. It was like a physical that anyone would do, but with a few extra items they wanted you to perform. These mostly centered on shoulder and torso flexibility. In addition to the vital signs being taken, blood drawn, testing with the eye chart, and checking overall physical condition, they put you through a series of shoulder movements designed to find limitations and pain.

The most concerning item facing pitchers and players alike was the possibility of having a damaged arm. It was up to the trainer to weed out signed players that could not perform the necessary tasks on the field. For myself, I already knew I started to have limited flexibility in my right shoulder and was aware I'd be given some of these tests.

Trainers always do both shoulders to see the difference between the shoulder you throw with and the one you don't. I made sure I didn't look too flexible in the left shoulder as I had already fully stretched out my right to get the maximum flexibility out of it. I just wasn't that flexible to begin with, and as far as I knew, that was their conclusion. I left the clinic with a clean bill of health and felt very relieved for doing so.

In Bob's case, he'd had arm issues for some time so getting through the physical wasn't a sure thing. He was always able to get by through shutting it down for an extra day or so, but we knew it'd be more challenging here in Arizona. The main issue he had was with his ulnar collateral ligament, or as it's commonly referred to, UCL. This is the most common problem with pitchers, as this ligament is the most susceptible to stretching and tearing. If it tears, the player will opt for a Tommy John surgery.

This surgery was named for the player who had the first such UCL replacement back in 1974 by Dr. Frank Jobe. There are some players who only stretch or partially tear this ligament. Some decide to rehabilitate the elbow and not have surgery. In most cases, they will eventually tear the ligament later in their career and then get the surgery.

In Bob's case, he'd always had some discomfort in the UCL ever since I met him in 1992. After each game pitched, he'd religiously ice down his elbow and shoulder for the prescribed 20 minutes. Even doing the right things to prevent injury didn't always go the way you wanted, and taking that extra day's rest always made you think maybe there was something awry. But that was recreational baseball—not preseason spring training for the Milwaukee Brewers. The next 60 to 90 days would really test how sound your arm was because you'd be throwing every day like you did in college.

Naturally, this was a source of anxiety for Bob and to some degree, me. We just did as most players do in that situation—didn't think about it and continued to do the things that got us there in the first place.

With the physical out of the way, it was time to focus on the task at hand and get ready to start throwing the next day. We got that done in the morning, which gave us the rest of the day off. It'd be the last day off for about a month, so we decided to not do anything strenuous and be ready for our first day. The place we were staying at was fairly comfortable with a pool and hot tub, and most of the players took advantage of that.

The majority of players were pretty lazy in general, so it wasn't surprising to see many of the younger players laying out around the pool by noon that day. We thought they were lacking a little gray matter because the Arizona sun over the next two months could prove to be a bit debilitating. Bob and I made sure to stay out of the sun and remain either in our quarters or the lobby area, watching television or playing cards.

Spades was generally the card game of choice for baseball players. During road trips, you'd always find two or three games going on. Any player in the minors would attest that spades could *almost* make the long ride bearable. Most of these guys in camp were veteran minor league guys, with a keen knowledge of 10 hour bus trips, so they were all pretty good players. We played spades pretty much most of the day and called it an early night so that we were ready to go on our first day of camp.

3 FIRST DAY OF SPRING TRAINING

There's always something special about the first day of spring training, whether you're a player, coach, or fan. It's that feeling of excitement that surrounds the ballpark and new hope for the fans, even Cubs fans, that their team will make it to the playoffs this year. The local markets for each team talk endlessly about what was weak about last year's team and if management did enough to fix it. You finally get to see some of the team's best prospects from last year and find out how much they have improved or regressed. And, of course, all the interviews of the team's star players. You hear their views on everything that happened last year and what they think of all the changes for this year. *This* spring training is going to be completely different.

The vast majority of players who sign a professional baseball contract do not get invited to a major league spring training. Dan Peltier, former MLB player with the San Francisco Giants and Texas Rangers, supported this fact through his testimony before a congressional committee on June 17, 1997.

In his words, "Only one out of every ten players that are drafted even gets one day in the major leagues, and only one out of a hundred actually has a career in the majors." His testimony was part of the fallout of the 1994 strike as Congress proposed legislation to apply anti-trust laws to Major League Baseball. For the few that get a chance to perform in a Major League spring training, an exhibition season was critical for many of these players. Many played for up to a decade and longer without one invitation to camp. These players were going to take this opportunity to finally get looked at. Just because they were going to camp didn't require them to play in "Scab Exhibition" games when they started. In fact, many of them said no when it came time to decide to play.

Some of those players, Tollberg for one, were accused and never given the chance to join the MLBPA. Because he was signed in a tryout to find replacements, he was viewed as a scab player by the union. He said he wouldn't play in the exhibition season and was still black-balled. He did manage to play a couple of seasons with the San Diego Padres before an injury cut his career short.

Brian got signed as a result of the search for replacement players, and this was the reason—in my opinion—why he was scourged by the union. Ed Durkin had signed him from the same tryout in Orlando, but not that day with the others. Bobby and I didn't even remember him from the tryout because his stuff wasn't that impressive other than his impeccable control. Still, Brian was only 22 years old with many more years to get signed and didn't want to blow his chances if the strike ended. Neither of us could possibly blame him and he made the best of his opportunity. I thought about what Brian must've been thinking and it must have been similar to the last time I tried to get signed by Durkin.

It was the spring of 1990; I was the pitching coach for St. Petersburg Catholic High School, and it was only a couple of years since turning Ed Durkin down after the Jacksonville game.

We'd always have game situations with the kids at the end of practice, and without fail, some of the kids wanted me to "heat it up" and try to hit against me. One particular evening, I was feeling pretty good and throwing to the kids was like something out of *The Rookie* where Dennis Quaid plays Jim Morris, former player with the Tampa Bay Devil Rays. Mike, the head coach, was puzzled when asking why I wasn't playing pro ball. Telling him my velocity wasn't good enough, he said to reconsider after that night. He believed the velocity was plenty good enough and said to give my friend a call.

So, that evening, I gave Ed a call. I hadn't spoken with him in months and after a few minutes of persuading him, he agreed to come out to the high school and put the gun on me. This chance would be redemption for the errors of my decision making in Jacksonville; showing something on Eddie's gun would send me to Helena.

It was a little surreal as the kids from the team gathered around to see me throw that evening after practice. Eddie didn't know Mike very well. St. Pete Catholic was not a baseball talent-laden school, so Durkin would rarely come to a game that involved the school. While warming up, they talked about last week and my velocity that evening. Things didn't feel right. I didn't have the same "pop" as the previous week. Sometimes it works out that way and the arm just doesn't get as loose, also the pressure of overthrowing can cause less velocity.

This would be yet another failed attempt for getting signed as my velocity did not reach above 85. I had prepared diligently for this moment. I took care of my arm and got plenty of sleep.

Eddie was getting fastball readings that were in the 83-84 mph range. They wouldn't sign me per his supervisor. It didn't really matter if you could get hitters out. They had to set certain standards, and one was your fastball had to reach 87-89 mph to get signed.

Think about trying to get into a specific college or university for a high school senior. A student may have proven that they are a hard worker and get outstanding grades, but their SAT and ACT scores are what gets them in. A student may have a 4.0 GPA, be class president and all that jazz, but if SAT scores are 1050-1150, they are not getting into an Ivy League school. They just have to make a cutoff point somewhere, and for me, I fell below the cut.

Although disappointed about the workout that evening, it didn't feel like it would be my last chance to try to get signed. I was having fun coaching high school; I would soon get a head job somewhere and progress like many of the college players from my generation do. Staying involved with baseball would be imperative, so coaching kept me in shape to play. There was even talk of a Senior Professional Baseball League starting up in the area. Players would have to be at least 30 years old and out of professional ball for at least a year. Maybe in five years or so, pitching in that league against some ex-pros would be at least something close to playing pro ball.

After playing with and against many players that made it to the show it was always the aspect of competing against them on the field that was the most appealing. When you play at a high level, you want to play against the best—and there's such a small margin at times when you look at the talent and luck involved. There are politics involved in professional sports just like major corporations—knowing somebody, getting an extra look, etc.

When Mike Piazza was signed in the 59th round of the draft by the Dodgers, it was because his father was friends with the upper brass of the organization. Give Piazza credit for excelling and making the best of his opportunity, because he may have never been given the chance without that favor. Many other players have been drafted and succeeded solely by being given a chance. Is that too much to ask?

Thinking about the past and all the chaos I went through from high school to USF really gave me perseverance when it came to challenges. I knew this task would be faced with many challenges, especially when it came to actually making the roster. I wasn't sure how I'd be received by the coaches, players, and the fans as we entered the facility at Dobson Ranch in Chandler.

After arriving, I soon learned what my ritual would be as I entered the locker room each morning. There was a check-in sheet that we signed each morning as we weighed in. The strength and conditioning (S/C) coach was usually there to keep tabs on this and checked in with us each day after practice. The S/C coach would give us small, short workouts to build the muscles surrounding the generally weak areas of our arms and shoulders from the time off over the winter. It was his job to snuff out any potential problems the players might have over the spring training period and to monitor players' use of anti-inflammatories, as those were an indication that they were in pain.

Spring training was like the first day of school all over again— players seeing each other after a long break, talking about how their vacation was and how this new season would bring hope to some of the guys that never had the opportunity to be here for spring training. Most of these guys had never been in this position, where they would get close personal attention from the coaches at the big league level. Still, a pall about the locker room had people wondering, "Who in the room here is going to be crossing the line to play in these games?"

Well, I certainly knew I was one of them, and by the way some of the others looked at me, I was sure they knew too. Every year there are always new players in the room at the start—the organization trades for players, releases players, signs players, and of course there is the draft. Unless you keep up with the organizational moves and know where they come from, you would have no clue on what was happening. The fact of the matter was that it was going to be an interesting six or seven weeks as this story would unfold underneath our feet.

These minor league players were all at different levels of their development within the organization, and some were on the early fast track to success. However, most were early in their career and not on the 40-man roster, which made them the most vulnerable to future issues with the current striking players. They needed to continue to play even when the others were striking, and the minor leagues provided this with other players that most likely never got an opportunity to play.

The system in place needed minor league baseball players to have a place for their prospects to play each year, and without it, there was no way they could get ready for the big club. These prospects use the step ladder to success, and it typically goes this way:

For a high school player drafted:

First year: Rookie or Low A baseball.

Second year: High A to AA baseball (There are different levels of A-ball, one is considered higher).

Third year: AA baseball most likely, and possibly AAA.

Fourth year: AAA with the hope of promotion to the 40-man roster in September.

Fifth year: Invite to spring training with the hope of making the team.

For a college drafted player:

First year: High A or AA baseball.

Second year: AA most likely, hopeful of promotion to AAA.

Third year: AAA with hope of promotion to 40-man roster (MLBs and the next 15 players in the organization).

Fourth year: 40-man roster, invite to spring training with hope of making the team.

This step ladder to success will vary for every high draft pick and especially for college players. It's not unusual for a high college pick to make it to the majors quickly. This happened to a teammate of mine at Florida State who won the Golden Spikes Award (NCAA baseball's equivalent to the Heisman Trophy) in 1986, Mike Loynd.

Mike was drafted in the second round by the Texas Rangers while Florida State was participating in the College World Series in Omaha, Nebraska. After the series was over, Mike was sent to AA Tulsa in the Texas League, where he performed well enough to be promoted on July 24, 1986 to the big club. In less than two months, Mike had been drafted and was playing in the major leagues.

It's certainly not your typical professional ballplayer's road to success, but it happened nonetheless. Unfortunately, Loynd was only in the major leagues a little over a year when he made his last appearance in 1987. Some believe his sudden rise into the Texas Rangers rotation was done prematurely and did not give him time to adjust to professional baseball.

The drafted player needs time to understand not only the rules and nuances of the game, but also to learn how to be a professional baseball player on the Major League level. Not that Loynd's career is unique—there are many players that didn't handle fame and notoriety well. Today, those players on the cusp of breaking into the majors go through seminars on how to handle the sudden changes that money and notoriety bring.

This system of promotion within the minor leagues facilitates and gives younger players time to learn and grow and has worked for decades. Still, you have to have minor leaguers that will never make the big club to make the system work.

Remember earlier how I said that 10% of the players know they're prospects and 20% of them know they will eventually be released? It's the 70% of the others that I want to speak about; 65% of them think they're prospects, but in reality only 5% are.

We finally got started with the Brewers' Manager Phil Garner and General Manager Sal Bando saying a few words before we started to stretch. Garner spoke to the players and mentioned the unusual circumstances that led us to this first day of spring training. He told us of his commitment to providing us with the best instruction as possible. Each player here would be treated with respect regardless of their individual situation and the camp would be run with that in mind. Bando added that he had an "open door" policy, and if there was any player who wanted to speak with him directly, all they needed to do was knock on his door.

Until the exhibition games were to start two weeks later,

players wouldn't have to decide whether they would cross the line or not. Some players attending that meeting were still undecided on what their decision would be and the next two weeks would be very hard for them.

The coaches and managers were in the worst positions for this labor stoppage. Nearly all the coaches in Major' League Baseball were former major league players. They certainly could both empathize and sympathize with the players and their decision to strike. However, these coaches worked for the owner and that made it sticky for them to keep their loyalty. The very same people who are trying to break the same union they were a part of for years and collecting pensions that had been negotiated.

Many of the coaches were part of the strike-shortened season of 1981, and this strike had more and hotter-contested issues on the table. The players deserved the loyalty of the coaches and managers, but they didn't pay their salaries, the owners did. Was this "open door" policy created by MLB in the weeks leading up to the first day, or was just something implemented by Milwaukee? My intuition is that it was a little of both.

The owners put in Bud Selig as the speaker for the owners and eventually the commissioner of baseball after the strike ended. Selig was the owner of the Milwaukee Brewers during the strike and acted as commissioner de facto. Baseball was in waters never seen before, and they needed some minor league players to cross the line for them to succeed. If the minor league player knew he would never reach "The Show," he may be more willing to cross.

By giving autonomy to the GM, it allows him to talk with the player and let him know where he stands in the organization. Then the player can evaluate and decide for himself. During peace times, the organization doesn't want the player to know what management thinks of him. Some will obviously know they are a prospect, but the vast majority will not.

There are many players in the minors that know they will never make the majors. They're just staying in as long as they can before having to go into the real world and get a job. That would indicate there are around 10% who know they're prospects in the organization and 20% or so "organizational minor league players" who know they will eventually be traded or released. This leaves about 70% of the minor-league players who most likely do not know how they fit into the organization.

It's that uncertainty of where we stand in the organization that keeps us going. With the "open door" policy these fringe players finally had the chance to talk to the general manager and find out if the organization really has them earmarked as a prospect. Why stay with a team if they have no intention of ever giving you the chance to play in the bigs? In the organization's mind, they believe this will make it easier for the players to sign the replacement contract and play in the exhibition games. The players realize they are going to eventually be released, anyway. This policy really had significance in regards to what happened when the players were given the documents to sign and play in the exhibition games.

When Bando said this, in my opinion, it meant that if players wanted to speak with him regarding how they fit into the organization, he'd let them know. A player could ask what management had in store for them in the long term and they would be given an honest answer. This was an unusual time, and that would never happen if the circumstances were not as they were. In two weeks, they would need to have players on the field for the first scab game against the Colorado Rockies in Tucson, and they needed to know who would cross.

After Garner and Bando had spoken to the players, it was time to get to work. This year was a bit different as both players and pitchers arrived on camp at approximately the same time. Usually, the pitchers and catchers would arrive a few days before the players, but the circumstances changed with the strike.

Spring training is a ritual that goes all the way back to high school days. It's a great feeling to get back to playing on the ballfield, but most players are over spring training within about a week. The higher the level of ball the longer the spring training season—high school took only three weeks, college four weeks, and professional ball around six weeks until the end. It's understandable though because each level has more dynamics than its predecessor, and more players to evaluate. From the team's perspective, it's an invaluable period to make decisions on where their players fit into the organization. For the players, it can mean any number of things ranging from a necessary evil to a proving ground. In all my years, it had always been that proving ground to make the statement of belonging there. Ever since my days of high school, trying to prove that I belonged on the playing field was a source of motivation.

4 WILTON

Growing up in the small affluent community of Wilton, Connecticut, certainly wasn't the easiest of roads to travel. Most of the kids had lived in Wilton their entire lives, while my family had moved there when I was in seventh grade. By high school, I had earned some respect as an adequate ball player, but I was by no means thought of as exceptional.

Adding to the equation was my attitude toward the game and my belief that I was a better player than what the coaches believed. My attitude was misinterpreted as conceited, and quite frankly, the coaches at Wilton didn't like it. It would be one of the biggest reasons for my success later on in college—the way I was treated in high school by the coaches.

Fairfield County, Connecticut is one of the wealthiest counties in the United States. At one point over the last decade, it was *the* wealthiest, and this gave the incoming freshman the ability to have their own baseball team. That made it easier to get much more playing time than most would get if they were competing with the other classes on the JV and varsity teams.

It's generally accepted as the unwritten rule in high school that sophomores will get less playing time than juniors, and so on. It's also understood that superior skill should at times override that. As a freshman, I had developed a relationship with the varsity coach for Wilton, Tenner Sterling.

Tenner thought I had a lot of talent and he was looking forward to working with me in the upcoming years. Generally unheard of at the time, there was a chance to possibly make the varsity team as a sophomore because of that relationship.

Shortly after starting my sophomore year in September, Tenner was fired and the JV coach Tim Eagen eventually replaced him. Eags (as he was affectionately called) for some reason never had a positive feeling toward me or my ability on the baseball field. He was also one of the football coaches for Wilton, a sport that I never really had the desire to play on an organized level.

I never was able to put my finger on why or what the problem Eagen had with me. Another thought was maybe he felt I was just too "cocky" in my ability to play. I felt a little overshadowed and let it be known my senior year. The circumstances were life-changing events. Eags, by the way, is still coaching at Wilton to this day and I wish him and the Warriors much success.

When Tenner was fired and replaced by Eagen, that was the end of any chance I had to play at the varsity level my sophomore year. With Eagen as the JV coach (and soon to be varsity coach), I played very little my sophomore year. There was the occasional pitching appearance and at bat without incident or fanfare.

There would be more opportunity next year as a junior. It'd

be best to wait my turn and not to make waves with a coach looking for reasons not to put you on the field.

After the high school season was over, I was able to actually play without all the political insert-your-own-adjective here. I wouldn't be judged by status, position in the community, family relationships with the coaches, etc. Your ability on the baseball field was all that mattered and the best players always played.

After the season was over, the all-star teams for each community were picked. Each area played neighboring communities to advance to state tournaments. Wilton never had the players to ever advance—most of the great athletes played lacrosse. With our town, baseball pretty much ended unless you were 16 and played American Legion ball. The rest of our summer consisted of stickball in Wilton until school started in September.

Stickball was very much like the street ball you would see kids playing in the streets of New York City. In Wilton, we had our own field with constructed fences, backstops, bases, and ground rules. It was the essence of summer with going to the field every day and playing until the sun went down. It was while playing stickball with my friend Brion and my brother Mike that I developed a love for baseball.

What great times we had there. Unfortunately, the field we played on has long been removed and was replaced by a major road. Even toward the end of the days we played there, the owner of the lot we used told us to stop. Because of the litigious society we now live in, baseball fields all across the country stay unoccupied during the summers.

Places like that just don't exist because of the paranoia of somebody suing somebody because they got hurt on their property. Baseball fields are locked and gated so kids can't go onto fields whenever they want anymore. That has much to do with why baseball participation has gone down over the past two decades in my opinion. It has become easier to play basketball or football because of the restrictions. We were fortunate to be given the chance to play without the restrictions, and it certainly made an impact on the rest of our lives.

My junior year in 1982 was filled with hope and excitement. I was playing baseball at a high level, and with my fastball reaching new heights, there were hopes of finally breaking through. As usual, March took forever to come, and spring tryouts started in the field house indoors.

The outside temperatures were still in the thirties and we wouldn't be going outside for at least two weeks. In fact, the final cuts for varsity would be made before we had even one practice outside. We took ground balls on the rubberized floor, hit into screens, and pitched on flat surfaces. This wasn't the most ideal situation, but we all knew what to expect.

In high school, most pitchers play another position when not on the mound. When I didn't pitch I would usually play third base and sometimes the outfield. Our starting third baseman was Doug Cuneo and he was one of Eags's favorite players. There was no intention of ever beating him out. It didn't matter how good I played, as it simply wasn't going to happen. Because I had an exceptional arm, I would play right field instead and just settle to back Doug up. It was my pitching that would cause no issues with making the varsity team this spring.

Over the next two weeks, everything seemed to be fairly uneventful, just like any other spring. I was surprised that nobody from the coaching staff ever spoke with me or took any time to see how I was doing. Even when pitching on the side, the coaching staff showed no interest.

With less than a week left until final cuts, I was getting a little uneasy. The coaches were simply ignoring me anytime I performed during the tryouts. They had broken down the tryouts into two groups that clearly defined one as JV, and one as varsity. Still participating with the varsity group, I thought nothing of the actions of the coaches during this last week. When the other pitchers would go and pitch, there would be someone working with them. When it was my turn, the coaches would go elsewhere.

"That's fine," I said. "Just because they don't like you and don't want to work with you doesn't mean they would sacrifice the betterment of the team."

Our team was lacking pitching depth to begin with, so I thought nothing of it for that reason, as well.

When the day came for the final cuts, I'm not even sure why I decided to look at the list. I wanted to see if Brion had made varsity because he was a long shot to make it. What was unexpected was the final list for varsity didn't have my name on it.

It has to be a mistake, without a doubt. I tried to speak with Eagen, but he wouldn't speak with me. I was told to go with the JV players to "tryout for that team."

Tryout? What does that mean? I thought.

The coaches for the JV team were Steve Shaw and David Roos. Shaw was by far the more influential of the two. I didn't know Shaw very well, but I knew his brother Doug, and his sister Sue was in my graduating class. Obviously, I was very upset about the entire situation, feeling like I was unjustly cast off because the coach didn't like me. Now I had to deal with having to prove myself on this team?

Well, at least Brion and my brother played on this team, so that made me feel a little better, but not much. There was one other player on the team who I felt was with about the same ability as me—Tom Newman.

At least we would have a pretty good starting pitching staff, I thought.

In high school, starting pitching staffs only needed two starters because we played two games a week and only had about 15 games all season. After a couple of days, I calmed down and accepted the fact about playing JV this season as a junior. Then, three days after being cut from varsity, the unfathomable happened. Shaw and Roos called me over and told me I was cut from the JV team.

I thought it was a joke.

"You're kidding me, right?" I said.

"No, we made the decision, and you will not be playing for us this season," Shaw said.

"How can you possibly cut me from the JV team? I'm one of the best players on this team, possibly the best!" I replied.

"We reserve the right to cut anybody on the team. You can tryout again next year!" Shaw bellowed with gratification.

"You can't cut me from this team. I refuse to be cut from this team. This will not end here and believe me, when I get back tomorrow I will have a spot on this team," I responded in disgust.

I left the field enraged at the situation these people put me in. They were trying to cut me for only one reason—they didn't like my cocky attitude on the field. I got into my 1969 Mustang and took off. I needed to be anywhere but near the baseball team at that moment. I just remember driving out of Wilton and down Route 33 into Ridgefield and never wanting to turn around.

It was quite possibly the most disappointing time in my entire life. I had never been cut by a baseball team before and didn't expect it to happen, at least not at this level. Not thinking clearly at this point (and not paying attention to the road or speed), the next thing I knew, there was a police cruiser with lights on behind me, as if things couldn't get any worse! Rollers!

That moment, the words of my father the previous year upon obtaining my license were bellowing in my ears.

"If you get one ticket, your driving privileges would be over," he said.

Luckily for me, the lady officer who pulled me over had a sympathetic ear. I think the statement, "worst day of my life" may have had a resonance to it as I held my head in my hands. She told me to go back home and stay off the roads if I couldn't concentrate on driving, letting me off with a warning.

After getting back home, I tried to understand what was going on in terms of the coaches on this team. They would rather have a player not feel he is better and be submissive on the field than one who is cocky and can get hitters out. I was under the impression that Coach Eagen had something to do with the JV cut. He was hoping it would put an end to my baseball career at Wilton and then he wouldn't have to deal with me anymore. Instead, it only fueled the fire that would spearhead the next four years of my life.

Attitude in baseball is a funny thing. My upbringing in Wilton (or more specifically, Fairfield County, Connecticut) made me realize a few things about life. Wilton is a very political town and many influential people live there. There were government officials, Fortune 500 CEOs, entertainers, actors, professional athletes, and many other dignitaries who called Wilton home. Growing up in that kind of town, one must learn how to play the political game. Knowing how to open up doors and play the game is crucial.

People who have lived there for generations have a level of respect to be able to open those doors with greater ease than those who are newer to the area. My family moved to Wilton specifically for the education my brother and I would receive. My parents never had the strong connections that many others had during those days spent in high school.

Struggling to make ends meet, we moved three times in six years while we were there. My parents decided to stay in Wilton rather than move to Bridgeport, Fairfield, or New Haven, where the rent would be cheaper. My parents had little or no political clout and never really fit into the Wilton social community.

The last few years, my father helped coach baseball on the Little League and senior league levels, and this did help his position in the community. These all were factors in why the events of my baseball days at Wilton High played out the way they did.

Every day was a struggle to prove I belonged and deserved to play this game regardless of outside influences. It was in this arena I learned that being "conceited" or "cocky" on a baseball field is a good thing. In high school, it was frowned upon to the point where you could get yourself cut.

In college and professionally, if you don't have it, you might as well hang up your spikes and go play softball somewhere, because that other guy you're facing has already beat you. Why? Because he is a "cocky SOB" and refuses to lose! That's how players get to those levels. They simply believe they are better than the other guys they're playing against. Coaches like Eagen and Shaw wanted the attention to be on them, not the players who make it happen on the field.

Well, I came back the next day after being cut from the JV team. I walked into their office and told them of my intentions.

"I'm not leaving this team unless you have a credible reason for cutting me," I said.

"Okay, if you keep your mouth shut and leave the coaching to us, you can stay," Shaw said.

"I'll let my play speak for itself. I don't need to talk to make an impact. We have a better chance of winning if I'm playing than if I'm sitting on the bench," I replied.

I ended up starting in right field for JV the entire season, and also pitched behind Tom Newman as the second starter.

Although I had a good season both in right field and pitching, I saw no action with varsity the entire year. Even when there was a player hurt and Eagen called someone up, I was overlooked for one of Eags's boys. The partiality and favoritism that Eags displayed was flat-out nauseating.

I couldn't say anything because of everything that had gone on earlier in the season. I had one more year to go, so I just sucked it up. It was again one of those things that fed the fire after finishing my senior year.

The next year was going to be better. I had a great summer season with the Wilton Reds, a 16- to 18-year-old youth summer team that many of the players from varsity played on.

My father had developed a relationship with some of the other non-high school coaches and was invited to coach with the Reds that year. Although I was only 16, I was the number two starter and pitched extremely well. We also played against many of the top players in the county, so it was a wealth of experience.

After the season was over, myself and two others were invited to play on the all-star team that would represent six towns in the immediate area. Ed Moore (one of the pitchers we had at Wilton) had to decline because of arm issues and took the summer off from playing baseball. The other was Casey Roy, who eventually played baseball at Lehigh University in Pennsylvania. We would play against other teams in a state tournament for a chance to play in the Babe Ruth World Series in Keene, New Hampshire.

The team was coached by Dick Prutting of Danbury, whose stepson Marc Thalman played at the University of Connecticut. Many of the players on this team played for the team he coached and obviously would get more opportunities to play.

Other towns represented were Ridgefield, New Canaan, Trumbull, New Haven, and Wilton. It would be the best team I'd ever been on to that point and getting playing time would be very difficult for me. Again, I knew if I just got the chance in practice to prove myself there would be an opportunity to play and to pitch. Soon after the practices started up, Casey decided not to participate because of not getting any real consideration for playing time.

It was apparent that the coach would primarily be playing his players from Danbury, and there would be little room for others to play. Casey felt the time sacrificed was not worth it, and quite frankly, I didn't blame him. I still felt positive and enjoyed being on a team with great talent. Again, just give me a chance to prove I can pitch on this team.

Finally, on a hot Saturday afternoon practice in Ridgefield, I would get my chance. We'd been practicing for a couple of weeks and just started to play scrimmage games to get ready for the qualifier in Stamford, so it was the perfect opportunity for me. We had some good pitchers on the team, but none I thought were better than me. Finally, I got the ball and started against our best lineup.

I pitched three innings that afternoon and did not give up a hit or a hard hit ball. I struck out the best players on the team and absolutely dealt. Even Tony Bellagamba from Ridgefield struck out and looked bad doing it against me. He'd hit a baseball about 450 feet last year against our JV team in my sophomore year.

I felt the coaching staff could be nothing but impressed and would want me as one of their starters. The entire rest of the summer, not one other pitcher we had on that team did better than I did that day. My enthusiasm was short-lived though, and Coach Prutting didn't make one attempt to put me on the mound the rest of the season.

To this day, I'm not sure why. I played against the best and I dominated. Again, my reward was to never see the mound again. Just unbelievable—couldn't make this stuff up!

Our team defeated the team from Stamford that summer, and we went to Keene, New Hampshire for the Babe Ruth World Series. We lost both games that weekend, one to Maine and the other to a team from Massachusetts. In two games, I played a couple of innings in the outfield with one at bat.

What was I doing that coaches treated me this disrespectfully? I played hard and with enthusiasm and joy. How could playing hard be considered disrespectful in a player/coach relationship? The only thing I could put my finger on was that he didn't want players from any other town except Danbury to excel on that team.

Sometimes the political game that coaches play can be to their own detriment. This team got to the series despite not playing the best players. We could have done better. Another coach to add to my list of people who placed obstacles in front of my ongoing quest to play the game I love.

Believe me, I will always appreciate how enraged I became due to the way these coaches treated me during high school and summer ball. Without that rage, I may have given up during my college days.

Even through being overlooked by the coaches at Danbury, I had progressed during the summer. My fastball was now in the mid-eighties, and my control was better than ever. I had some control issues during this time, but always seemed to get out of trouble because of the good slider. Still, I wanted to have a pitching coach that could do more than telling us to run, but that was not the case.

Our pitching coach at Wilton was Mark Ketley. His experience was pitching for Southern Connecticut State College a few years earlier. There was really no coaching involved with Mark—he was more like a babysitter than anything else. When it came to coaching, he offered nothing for me and my pitching. He would say this was a good pitch and that was a bad pitch, but offer little to help me correct any issues. He was a left-handed pitcher and was more interested in helping Tom Newman on the pitching staff.

Tom was a lefty with a big, sweeping curveball, which was a very pretty pitch indeed. He was a junior in 1983, and considered our best chance to win games when he was on the mound. Tom had lived in Wilton all his life and was the pitcher in Little League that once struck out all 18 players he faced. His family was very well-known, and he was given every opportunity to succeed. More than anything else, he was favored by the Wilton High School coaching staff. Tom was hoping to play in Division I and eventually played for Le Moyne College. Le Moyne was Division II until they turned Division I in 1988, Newman's last year there.

We also had senior Ed Moore on the staff as the number two starter. Ed was very well-liked on the team, and more importantly by Coach Eagen. Eags was Moore's coach on the Wilton football team and had a close relationship with Ed's parents. Ed eventually blew his arm out his senior year due to Eagan overusing him during his time at Wilton. Moore went on to Furman University where he was going to play, but with his inability to throw a baseball without pain, he decided to hang it up. I often wonder how good a college player that Ed could have been if Eagan had learned how to use the other players on the team instead of overworking him. It's just a shame.

With all this, I was the number three option for the pitching staff. This wasn't much to celebrate, considering the public's opinion about Wilton High School baseball in general. We were last in the Fairfield County Inter Athletic Conference (FCIAC) in 1982 winning only four games and losing 16, and there was little to believe we would fare much better.

In December of 1982, our team had the opportunity to attend the Bucky Dent Baseball Camp in Delray Beach, Florida. A few of the players decided to go down and attend the camp. Ed Moore, Tom Newman, JJ Russo and I took the flight down and had a chance to learn more about the game—and hopefully get some exposure. JJ was a sophomore and had a bright future for Wilton as a starting pitcher before he graduated in 1985.

For most of the players, it was the trip to Florida during the winter months that was great. The camp loved to make money from the rich kids in Fairfield County, and there were many parents more than happy for a vacation, too.

The trip was offered to all the schools in the county, so we saw many of the guys we played against in high school while we were there. This was also an opportunity to see what some of the scouts thought of my ability and aspirations of playing major college baseball.

Florida was one of the hotbeds, along with California, Arizona, and Texas when it came to college baseball, so who better to ask than some of the scouts attending the camp? I remember one of them was a scout for the Red Sox, Phil Rossi. He was looking for players that may have fallen between the cracks. He was evaluating the players that came from all over the country, not just his territory in the northeast. During this time, I made sure to try to get his attention when possible and then get an honest opinion on how I measured up to other players going into college.

I finally had the chance to talk with him the day before camp ended and was excited to hear what he had to say. I gave a good showing on my ability and would certainly be able to play against others in at least Division II. Phil told me I'd be lucky to play Division III or NAIA. According to him, the talent pool was too overwhelming and many deserving players don't even get the chance when given an opportunity.

I was perplexed by his comments. I knew he was a respected scout and been with the Red Sox for a couple of years—but Division III? NAIA? My dream was to play at either Arizona State or Florida State because they were the two best baseball schools when I was growing up. *Was I giving myself too much credit for what I believed my ability to be? Was I really just an average baseball player when compared to other high school seniors playing around the country? After all, last year I got cut from JV as a junior. It doesn't get much lower than that, so maybe I'm not that good.* Another kick in the groin is really what it felt like, and again, I was on the outside looking in.

I pondered for a while and made the most of Rossi's comments, trying to figure out why he said them. I figured he was honest with me and truly believed his words and I really wasn't a Division I player. *It's time to stop listening to those people and start believing in yourself*. They can't see what is inside of your heart and mind—forget those people and try your best.

After getting back from Florida, I decided not to listen to people anymore when it came to the direction of my life regarding baseball. In my mind, I was good enough to play at a high level. I wouldn't let anybody say things to discourage me. My last year of high school baseball would be starting soon, and

I wanted to be in the right frame of mind when it came time to play.

I had talks with my parents about what colleges to attend after I graduated. I applied to University of Florida, Florida State University, University of South Florida, and University of North Florida in December and hadn't heard from any of them—it was January. Florida State was obviously my first choice and Florida was doubtful, being an out-of-state applicant. I got acceptances from both South Florida and North Florida, but rejections from UF and FSU. As it would play out, this ended up as a blessing in disguise.

One of my friends in Wilton was Jeff Wirz, who had a connection with South Florida. His father, Robert, was an advisor for then-Commissioner of Baseball Bowie Kuhn. Every year, they attended the Hall of Fame inductions, and the head coach at South Florida was the famous Philadelphia Phillies HOF pitcher Robin Roberts.

Remember my explaining of the political nature of Wilton and all the influential people who live there? Never once in this town was I able to use it to my advantage, and all of a sudden it fell into my lap. After being disappointed by FSU, I was determined to make this opportunity work.

Naturally, I accepted the offer from South Florida and asked Jeff's father to write a letter to Coach Roberts about me playing for the Bulls. The letter said nothing about giving me a scholarship or preferential treatment—just the opportunity to be given an extra look when it came to tryouts in the fall. And that was that! It was all set before we had even had our first practice my senior year. I knew where I was going and that I'd be given a shot to make the team as a walk-on.

I couldn't ask for anything more. USF is a Division I school, played in the Sun Belt Conference, and had a respected coach that was a Hall of Fame pitcher. If I could make the team, what better person to learn how to pitch from than someone in the Hall of Fame?

Eventually, baseball started up for my senior season, and as usual, we were in the field house for the first two weeks. No question I was going to be on varsity this year; word had gotten out about my summer, and I was much improved. Even Eags was impressed with my performance at the baseball camp in Florida, and that solidified a starting position in right field. That being said, I'd be the third starter on a team that only needed two.

By now, word started getting out about the colleges we were going to attend and Coach Eagen was asking us where we were going next fall. Most everybody in the gym knew that for the seniors it was their last year playing organized baseball. With the exception of Ed Moore, nobody else was thought to have a chance to play. That included me.

Finally, Eags got to me.

"I'm going to the University of South Florida in Tampa," I announced proudly.

"Yes, isn't that where they have that new 'Sun Dome'?" Eagen replied.

"Yes, they do. It looks pretty neat!" I said.

"And you're gonna play baseball there, too—right, Ed?" Some other player in the group said sarcastically.

"Yes, I'm going to try," I calmly said through my controlled anger.

After my response, I heard a few chuckles amongst the team. I never knew who it was that said those words, which I still hear to this very day. It is amazing how a few callous words by some ignorant individuals can lead to inspiration. More people to add to my list.

The beginning of the season started for us with a practice

game against Weston, one of the towns nearby. They weren't in our conference, so we wouldn't play them during the regular season. The baseball camp we attended in Delray Beach was very helpful for me as Coach Eagen was there, too. During the batting practices I had there, I was hitting the ball very well, and Coach seemed to notice my newfound power. Maybe it was just the anger, and I was taking it out on the ball. Either way, Eagen moved me up to 5th in the order right behind our best hitter, Ed Moore.

During the game, I hit the ball to left center field over everybody's head. If there were fences, it would've clearly left the yard. Unfortunately—like most fields in Connecticut—they didn't have fences, and you had to run it out. I eventually got tagged out at home by the catcher, and as I approached the bench (there was no dugout), only Brion came to greet me with a "nice hit."

For the first and only time, Eagen came out and yelled at the team for not giving me any support after my hit. Most of the team didn't think much of me and didn't like my conceited attitude on the field. Off the field I was a quiet guy, but on the field, it was the opposite. Well, regardless of Eagan's rant, things wouldn't change during the rest of the year.

Even after Eagen finally supported me, it didn't mean he was in my corner, either. The team as a whole didn't have much talent according to people "in the know." The players were good, just not properly utilized by the coach, and some weren't playing the position that would optimize the team's talent. And yes—there were players that Eagen would play even though there were better options for winning. In my opinion, he knew they weren't going to win much, so why put a better player in to replace another when you have a relationship with the parents?

And so it goes with the political saga of Wilton sports. It was hard to imagine that it could get worse, but it did. After some initial success in the beginning of the season and winning a couple of games, things looked brighter for the team. The local paper for our small community was a publication from Acorn Publishing called the *Wilton Bulletin*.

The *Bulletin* was a weekly publication that many small communities had during this time. They wrote human interest stories plus what was happening around the community. Acorn did these community newspapers in New Canaan, Ridgefield, Weston, Westport and a few other towns in the area. Just like any other paper they had a sports section that talked about the high school sports for each school.

The sports editor at the time was a gentleman named Reid Walmark. Walmark was the person who handled the writing and editing for each of these publications, which were distributed to the communities. Each Wednesday, the players on the team would get the *Bulletin* to see if they got their name in the paper for the previous week's baseball games at Wilton. Like any other high school kid, it's cool when you get your name mentioned in a publication.

I was particularly fond of this as well, and even had my picture printed before the start of the regular season as one of the potential starters. I wanted to read each Wednesday with the rest of the guys.

One particular Wednesday, I was looking forward to seeing what was written about the previous week's games. We had a game against one of our rivals, the Norwalk Bears, and I relieved Tom Newman, who hadn't faired very well that game. I came in relief and basically limited the damage against the Bears. I finished the game giving up a couple of hits over the last few innings.

Newman had lost the game 9-1 and didn't look good doing it.

We all have those days when nothing you do works, and it happened to be that day for Newman. What I read was a completely different account of what transpired that afternoon. The *Bulletin* stated that I had started the game and gave up all the runs and Newman came in relief and stopped the bleeding I'd caused.

I couldn't believe my eyes when I read this account in the paper! It must've been a mistake. They couldn't possibly have erred that badly to confuse the two of us ? To make matters worse, there was an additional article about our upcoming game against our rival, Ridgefield. The article stated that unless Newman was on the mound, we'd have no chance of beating them. Well, so much for my ability to pitch and beat a good team like Ridgefield.

This was simply unacceptable in my mind, and I wanted to set the record straight. I needed to let the *Wilton Bulletin* know they made a mistake and reported incorrectly. People make mistakes, not a big deal in the grand scheme of things—right? Journalists have opinions and so do players. I felt we'd beat Ridgefield with me starting and considered this an insult.

Thursday afternoon after school, I called the *Bulletin* and informed them of the error. I let them know that we had an excellent chance to beat Ridgefield if I started the game pitching. Someone from the *Bulletin* spoke with me for about five minutes, and it was a cordial exchange. There was no yelling or going back and forth. I stated that the *Bulletin* incorrectly reported the line score and switched us , then alluded to the article about Ridgefield and that I felt strongly about being able to beat them if I pitched. That was it, harmless enough, right? Wrong!

Next Wednesday, the day the new *Wilton Bulletin* came out, and we had an away game. As everybody on the team prepared to leave, a bellowing voice from outside the bus yelled, "Porcelli, get the hell out here!"

It was Eagen, and he was livid. I hadn't read the article in the paper as of yet because we'd just gotten out of school. The *Bulletin* baseball headline read, "Wilton Baseball getting better, but still attitude problems on the team."

Getting off the bus, I knew instantly why he wanted to speak with me. I also knew this would be a "one-way" conversation.

"What the hell gives you the right to call into the *Bulletin* about an article? If you have a problem with something in the paper, you are to speak with me—*only* me," Eagan said.

He wanted to know what gave me the right to call the *Bulletin* and start mouthing off at them. I was certainly going to pay the price because of my actions. At the time, I was petrified, and couldn't move a muscle. I can't remember the game we had that day or whether I even played. When we got back, I was able to get a copy of the *Bulletin* to read what was written.

The article spoke about an unnamed player who called in to the *Bulletin* to tell them about an error they made. The article stated I was disrespectful and then "berated" them for making the mistake.

Wait—that wasn't what I did. I simply told them about the mistake. I didn't yell, or in their words, "berate" them. I just spoke matter-of-factly about the situation.

The article went on, "We found that we made an error in reporting and for that error, we apologize."

Well, at least they admitted to making the error. I read further and looked for the forthcoming correction, but the article ended. Where's the correction?! They never even told the readers what the error was. Unbelievable! Was it deliberate?

It was clear to me that they must have known what they were doing. Admitting they made a mistake, but not let any of the readers know what the mistake was must be deliberate.

Again, what did I do to deserve this disrespectful behavior? I wasn't disrespectful in any manner and was always cordial whenever possible. Why was I being singled out? Am I supposed to "take one for the team" because Tom was considered the best hope to play at the next level? Would an article like this hurt his chances? Since when was correctly reporting news such a dangerous thing?

I've thought about that day when summoned by Eagen and I'm not sure if any of the players knew the circumstances that surrounded it. I believe most thought that it was my ego that got in the way. I couldn't handle anything bad being reported about me, whether it was true or not. So much for my first lesson in dealing with the press.

Dealing with the media can be a very tricky thing. I can certainly understand the stance of why some players refuse to talk. Their quotes could be taken out of context, only writing certain things to create the illusion of the writer's perspective and not what the player intended to say. I felt the distrust at an early stage and had to be reprogrammed to believe that most journalists and media are people and try to do the right thing.

For over 30 years, I held the writer and editor, Reid Walmark, primarily responsible for misreporting the game against Norwalk. I finally corresponded with Mr. Walmark and learned that he'd reported what Tim Eagen told him to report. Eagen called in the game that Walmark didn't attend, and credited me with the start and loss and Newman with cleaning up after.

Although I had called the *Bulletin*, I never spoke directly to Mr. Walmark. I can only hypothesize this fact. Walmark never got the facts of that game and spoke with Eagen after I called in. Eagen then told Reid that I was the problem and there were no errors in the report—and he'd handle the situation with me.

Eagen's abrasive, in-your-face personality could be very intimidating for anybody, including a 26-year-old local sports journalist. The last thing Reid Walmark was going to do was get on Eagen's bad side.

I was back in Wilton recently to learn that Tim Eagen is still coaching on the football and baseball teams. I had the opportunity to be in his space, but he declined to acknowledge my presence. I was disappointed, but not surprised. Some things will never change.

We did have a few light moments during my final year in Wilton. It was December and South Florida was having a heat wave during the time we were at the baseball camp. Temperatures in the 80s and sunny skies added up to disaster. Vacationing from New England and not being used to the intense sun in Delray Beach made for a bad combination. We didn't heed the advice of the counselors and ended up with blisters all over our faces. We were quarantined to the hotel for at least one day and possibly more. Naturally, with nothing to do, we had to occupy our free time by partaking in some sophomoric hijinks! Well, no experience drinking like the others from Wilton wasn't going to keep me from partaking.

It didn't take long for Moore to go down to the local store for some cheap beer and a set of dice to play a game called Mexican. My life up to that point had been pretty sheltered, quiet, and stayed on the conservative side for the most part. Most of the free time in high school was spent involving myself with baseball, and drinking had never been a thought. That was about to end.

I figured that I might as well lighten up a little bit. Moore was the best baseball player in Wilton and it'd probably be good for me to show a different side of myself. The beers flowed and we all had a good time for the next hour or so. There was a common bond that we were in this together. Despite the differences we had from each other, we had a time to call our own, and it felt good.

After a while, the beer was gone and this led to the trivial nonsense that can sometimes lead to cruelty. Our hotel was situated along US 1 in Delray with a great view of the cars rolling northward on that hot sunny day. One poor fellow happened to be riding his bike in the lane designated for him shortly after we had run out of beer with nothing to do. This fellow was precariously balancing about 300 oranges on his bike and paying more attention to that than anything else.

During the time we lived in Wilton, kids found humor in yelling, "Sir?" to see if you could get their attention. I'm not sure why it was entertaining, but it was nonetheless. In this particular case, JJ decided to add a little flair by saying, "Sir, you dropped one..." from the second floor balcony of the hotel.

That one statement sent this poor guy flying as he hit the curb looking for the one orange that obviously didn't drop. Oranges were everywhere, cars trying to avoid hitting them, bike on the ground, and one puzzled, pissed-off bicyclist with a huge cleanup effort in front of him.

As insensitive as the act was, it was one of the funniest moments I have ever encountered. This poor fellow spent 20 minutes picking up all the oranges. Once again he had balanced, and one false statement by someone with bad intentions could send him flying. Never again would he get sucked into someone fooling him.

He finally started back down the road with everything set in place.

JJ yelled out to him," Hey Mister, you left one over there..."

Sure enough, the poor guy almost bit the dirt again, but recovered without crashing to the ground. What we did to that poor guy was inexcusable, but it certainly entertained us as we recovered that day in Delray.

We finished the season that year only winning four games, just like the previous year, and nobody really noticed, anyway. The lacrosse team won yet another state championship, our 14th in 15 years. Everybody was happy in Wilton despite the poor baseball record.

I often wonder how good our team would've been if we had some of the players who opted for lacrosse instead of baseball. One player, JB Clarke, could have probably been an All-State selection as a pitcher and played Division I with ease, but played lacrosse instead. Presently, JB is the lacrosse head coach for Limestone College, and won his second Division II championship in 2015. Way to go, JB!

Like many of the lacrosse players, they became elite college players and coaches in Division I. One player from Wilton, Mike Pressler, was the coach of the Duke Lacrosse team through the mid '90s. To this day, Wilton Lacrosse will be king and baseball a distant second each springtime in New England.

Now that I'm 50 years of age, I look back on the people, places, and memories of Wilton, Connecticut. Our graduating class of 1983 still gets together every five years and has a blowout for a reunion. Many of those fellow students that I never really got to know, I have become good friends with over the years. I'm extremely thankful that I've been able to stay in touch with all of them through various methods, and as we move on to the later stages of life I am looking forward to meeting them all again when the chances arise. In closing, "Way to Be, '83!"

5 UNIVERSITY OF SOUTH FLORIDA

My time with WHS baseball was over. It was time to concentrate on getting ready for the fall and the tryout with the University of South Florida. I was still playing for the Reds and had been solid as a starter for them all summer. Making the USF team would require even more improvement, and there were only a few more games.

During the summer, USF had an orientation where the students prepared and took placement exams to start fall classes. My main focus would be making the baseball team, but that had very little to do with what they had in mind.

Recruited players who enter schools with an athletic scholarship have it much easier. There are no issues getting the classes you want; they get submitted before the graduate students. An academic adviser can help with your schedule, and free tutors are at your disposal. Classes are arranged around the team's schedule so you are available to be on the field for practice.

Incoming freshman have it the worst. They are the last to pick their classes, so what's needed may not be available. If you didn't get the class you needed, most likely you'd probably stand in drop/add all day. They also could expect to have classes spread out all over the day. I do not envy the incoming freshman, that's for sure!

Orientation was not only for what college life would be like, but also what living in Florida would be like. Tampa in the middle of June can be a cornucopia of weather patterns, and we learned that the day we arrived. Because my folks were moving down to Tampa, Dad would be looking for a place to live while I was attending the orientation.

There are three main bridges that connect Tampa to St. Petersburg. That day, we started to cross one of them in clear skies that soon turned dark. We ran into a blinding rainstorm in the middle to clear skies exiting the other side. That is a typical summer day in Tampa!

After getting settled in and taking a few placement exams for orientation it was time to meet my next coach, Hall of Fame pitcher Robin Roberts.

Words could not express my excitement entering the Sun Dome for the first time! The baseball offices were in the Sun Dome, as were the baseball locker rooms. This would be a place I would become very familiar with and hopefully soon. Unfortunately, Coach Roberts was not there at the time, but assistant coach Eddie Cardieri happened to be there.

After introducing myself, I wanted to get as much information on how the tryout process worked. I let Coach Cardieri know about the recommendation from one of Coach Roberts' associates. I embellished a little bit, but what could it hurt? I was still ignorant about how tall the odds were of actually making this roster, but any little bit helped.

Cardieri informed me that walk-on tryouts would be held shortly after classes started in August and to keep an eye out for the announcement. The impromptu meeting lasted about three minutes, and that was it. Another mission accomplished. At least he will remember me at the tryout, and that wouldn't be a bad thing. Every year in Wilton we had tryouts, so I was used to that already, how much different could it possibly be?

Leaving the Sun Dome that afternoon, there was a feeling like this was a place where I could make a difference. Maybe it wasn't Florida State, but it was still Division I. Florida State was on the schedule; they played each other three times in 1984 and another three in 1985. I would get the experience of seeing the team I dreamed about in person! If things worked out, maybe I would even have the chance to pitch against them. *Wait, check yourself. Let's put our goals in perspective here. Let's get a uniform first and then worry about getting on the mound.*

There! Set your priorities in order and attack your goal, that's the ticket to success. Okay, time to get to know a few people before we head back to Connecticut!

The last night in Tampa for orientation gave me the chance to see what college life would be like. That evening was my first college party. I wasn't much of a drinker in high school, which meant I never drank. Our escapades during the Delray baseball summer camp involved some drinking, but that was my entire experience in high school. Parties were something completely new to me. Meeting a few people and getting acquainted with the university was a key. It helped my psyche and made me excited to get back to Tampa in August. It wouldn't be long to make that trip down from Connecticut and settle into the Tampa Bay area.

Finally, we packed up our belongings and headed down to

the Tampa Bay area. My parents had made arrangements for employment, and everything was looking good as we headed off in early July. We got to Tampa a few days later and settled down at a modest duplex in central Clearwater near the west coast. We had sold all our belongings, and we were "all-in" committed after they'd left their jobs in Connecticut.

Even the best laid plans don't work the way you want them to, and sometimes they're forced upon you. After all the hard work my parents had put in to solidify a place in the community for employment, both of them were denied the positions after we arrived in Florida.

After all was said and done, they hadn't signed any contract or employee agreement before picking up and moving. This left them with no recourse against the employer. In many ways, I'm the same type of trusting person they were. The days when a handshake was as good as gold were long since gone. The next few years they would struggle for work and they said nary a word to me of the situation they were in at the time.

Starting school at USF had an unexpected surprise in the first class I attended. My calculus class had a familiar face as somebody from Wilton was there, Scott Reading! Although he was a year ahead of me, I knew his brother Mark from a few of my classes.

Knowing someone else from Wilton helped me adjust to the sudden acceleration of material as a college student. Anything that helped me adjust was fine by me. The schedule was imperative to have no afternoon classes as the baseball team would be practicing then. It also helped having one night class each Wednesday for three hours. This class started after we were already done with practice, and the other classes were in the mornings. We would help each other during the semester and eventually travel back up to Connecticut for Christmas break.

The tryouts were larger than anything in Wilton High. There must have been two hundred students trying out and most of them weren't going to make the spring team. Generally, you would see some guys make the fall team for scrimmages, and they'd fall by the wayside in the spring. It's all about making the spring roster because you're not officially on the team unless you make the spring team. Making the spring roster didn't even guarantee you'd travel with the team in the spring, either. Some scholarship athletes don't even make the travel squad.

During the three-day tryout, many thoughts were going through my head, most having to do with the uphill battle to make the spring roster. *Will this be my last time playing organized baseball? What will I do if they cut me?*

Coach Roberts watched me closely in the bullpen during the tryouts. Throwing very hard, mid to high 80s was required to play at this level for a right-handed pitcher. He liked what he saw during those three days and decided to keep me aboard.

I stayed on for the rest of the fall, and was given every opportunity to make the spring team. Most of the fall we scrimmaged but we also played junior college (JUCO) teams as well. From the walk-on tryouts, they kept about seven guys for the fall, and only two would play during the spring season. Joe Hunter was one of those seven guys and, unbeknownst to me at that time, he'd play a significant role in my baseball involvement over a decade later.

Joe was an excellent pitcher from Pinellas County, Florida, and was at USF getting his degree to eventually work in the medical field. Already in his third year, this was his final attempt to make the spring squad. The past two years, he'd had a few bumps in the road due to some injuries.

He had been a starter at Pinellas Park High School in Largo,

Florida. Pinellas Park had an excellent baseball team and to be considered the top pitcher at a large school from Pinellas County, Florida is a great credential, indeed!

Joe had excellent control and was very bright when it came to understanding how to pitch. Joe was also fortunate that his neighbor growing up was Larry Bowa of the Philadelphia Phillies. Larry would invite him to functions at his house when some of the other Phillies were over during spring training. Mike Schmidt, Greg Luzinski, and others would fish in the pond out behind Bowa's home, and Joe would learn from some of the greats of the game.

After Joe graduated and became a pharmaceutical drug representative, he stayed around the game and was even offered by the Phillies to be a roving pitching coach. This coach would visit the minor league teams and tutor the pitchers in each minor league city. Unfortunately for Joe, the pay was far less than his current salary with his employer at the time, and he had to decline.

I was really hoping that Joe would make the team that year, but his efforts, along with his injuries, caused him to leave the team before the fall season concluded. Although we spent time on and off the field to that point, I wouldn't see Joe again until many years later.

Making the fall team at USF was the first step to making the spring team. I've always believed you need to set realistic goals when attaining what is perceived unattainable. Every young boy playing in his first games in Little League dreams of being a MLB player when he grows up. Each level in sports requires more dedication, talent, and luck to not only play, but have success to get to the next level. There were no "cuts" in Little League unless you spoke of the All-Star teams that participate in the annual tournament to qualify for the Little League World Series in

Williamsport, Pennsylvania.

It obviously gets different in high school. Most of the players eventually get cut, and half of the players on the team get very little playing time. The starting players have the vast majority of the time on the field and the rest sit.

Most of the "recreational players" are done playing baseball by the time they reach 16 years old. According to the High School Baseball Web, those good enough to be a starter for a high school team and a senior had about a 6% chance of playing at the collegiate level.

This 6% is comprised of players that play in Divisions I through III, junior college and NAIA in the NCAA, and decreases over the next four to five years of the student-athlete's career for that school. Of the approximate 30,000 NCAA baseball players, about 6,500 are seniors. About 10% of them will sign a professional contract with MLB through the draft or as a free agent.

Once they sign that contract, they are usually sent to a lower minor league team in Rookie or Low A league to start their journey to possibly make the Major Leagues. Less than 10% are successful in making that trek.

Back in 1983 trying out for the University of South Florida Bulls Division I team there was no conception of these daunting numbers against me. My desire was to play baseball at the highest level possible, so simply making the team was the only thought.

During the fall season, I felt myself starting to settle in with the rest of the USF team quite well. Many of the players on the team would later be drafted and played with future MLB players in the Tampa area. Dwight Gooden, Gary Sheffield, Tino Martinez, and Luis Gonzalez were just a few of the players who had played in a Tampa high school within the previous two years.

One player on USF was a freshman catcher from the Clearwater area, Scott Hemond. When I first met Scott, I thought he was a senior because the guy was so big! He was the prized recruit for Coach Roberts and a surefire first-round pick by the time he would be a senior.

Hemond was the best defensive catcher in NCAA baseball as a freshman, with an eye-popping arm that was simply incredible. He was timed at 1.7 seconds getting the ball from home plate to second base, which is well above average for MLB. When one was pitching, and an opposing player would try to steal second base, one had better get out of the way of Scott's throw because it would hit you in the mid-section. In fact, that first year during the spring of 1984, Scott threw out the NCAA stolen base record-holding Lance Johnson of South Alabama four of five times by a minimum of three feet. The only stolen base Johnson had was when the fielder dropped the ball by accident! Johnson would go on to steal many bases for the Chicago White Sox after leaving college.

Another of my teammates was senior Ken Ericksen. Kenny was one of Coach Roberts's best and most studious players. He later became the USF woman's softball coach. Ken's success as a woman's college softball coach would give him the job of the Woman's Olympic Coach for USA. I was fortunate enough to be Ken's roommate on the road in 1984 and learned a great deal about being a college player and teammate. He was also from the Northeastern part of the country, New York, and understood the area of my upbringing. The Northeast was hardly the area for baseball talent and few from there ever play in college, so having him there made things easier for me.

Very quickly, I was put into a long relief role that is usually earmarked for those who need to prove themselves before participating in high leverage situations. The coaches determined that I had a strong arm, was never tired or sore, and always took the ball when asked. Even more importantly was the infectious desire to have fun on the baseball field. This was always considered a positive trait.

I pitched in many scrimmages (and also against JUCO teams) that fall, and had more strong outings than bad ones. The coaches worked on my delivery and developed a change-up, which was also significant in my future development.

Eddie Cardieri's brother Ron who was the pitching coach for the Bulls taught me that pitch. Ron was a former catcher for the Florida Gators, and after being drafted by the Baltimore Orioles in 1981, played two seasons in the minors. Many times I had thought what it would be like to actually have a pitching coach who would teach me pointers on how to pitch, learning new pitches, etc.

What a difference six months make! Ron made me think about pitching; how to set up hitters and think ahead, he was the perfect first pitching coach for me. Not that having a Hall of Famer as the head coach to learn pitching from was less than average, but Ron was closer to our age and translated better to us than Coach Roberts.

One of the most surreal events at USF ever experienced was with Joe Hunter during the fall season off the baseball field and in the locker room after practice one afternoon. Local TV Channel 8 News was out at the ball field that day doing promotional pieces for cut-ins during television shows and news broadcasts. These were generally five seconds and designed to fill gaps during airtime throughout the day. For example, the camera crews caught me snapping a ball in the air, making it spin. This was a drill I practiced to get better rotation on a curveball. The cameramen thought it looked cool, so they filmed me doing it. After completing the move, they told me to look into the camera and give a thumbs up saying, "Bulls Baseball, catch it!" It ended up a couple of times on the air, so that was pretty neat for an 18-year-old to watch on television.

Later that day after practice, Joe and I heard the "clip-clop" of high heels walking on the terrazzo floor in the bathroom area of the locker room while we were showering!

Joe said, "What the hell is that?"

We peered out of the shower to see Gayle Sierens, the Channel 8 sports anchor, interviewing Scott Hemond, who was wearing nothing but a towel.

Sierens was very well known at the time because she was one of the few women in the news that was the sports anchor. In many ways, she was one of the pioneers of women in the NFL. Along with Jayne Kennedy and Phyllis George, Sierens helped the infiltration of women in NFL broadcasts that have many of the beautiful sideline reporters you see during the game. Sierens certainly understood what it took to not only get the story, but went to great lengths to make a statement doing it back in the '80s while earning her stripes. Later that year in 1984, she was awarded a Florida Emmy for Best Sports Reporting in the Tampa market. She did end up parlaying her work on Channel 8 by getting a stint with NBC Sports in 1987. Sierens became the first female sports reporter to do play-by-play for an NFL game, which was between the Seattle Seahawks and the Kansas City Chiefs on December 27, 1987.

Well, Gayle had been around the facility over the past couple of days. We had already seen her interview Scotty at least once on the field, so Joe was a bit skeptical about Sierens having to interview him again. To this day, he's convinced that Sierens had a thing for Scotty. Anyway, it was a surreal experience to have a woman reporter walk by while showering. Looking back, I would have to say it was a bit disconcerting!

As the fall season ended, I felt very secure about making the spring team, and this was confirmed as we went off for Christmas break. Scott Reading made arrangements to head back up to Connecticut for the four-week layover before classes started up again. On the trip up, we'd have a stop at Duke University where his brother Mark was attending school.

Visiting Duke University was remarkable in the sense of it being not only a great academic school, but a gorgeous setting in the hills of North Carolina. My grandfather, Paul Shipley, had attended Duke back in the '30s and played football there. It would've been great to have played baseball at Duke, but my grades in high school wouldn't have been good enough.

Duke was everything college should be. It had tradition, atmosphere, and spirit—just walking by Cameron Indoor Stadium gave me chills knowing the tradition of Duke Basketball. USF was a good school both academically and athletically, but lacked that "old school" college feel. Duke was the number one desired university for the 1983 Wilton High School seniors, and nine of them chose to attend the school in Durham.

Visiting Duke left an everlasting impression just by stepping on the campus. The gothic architecture and rolling hills among the Carolina pines was an awesome sight! Students walking through such a beautiful, historic campus must be inspired. These students were fortunate to study in such a perfect venue of landscape and history. USF is a respected university and one of the best in cancer research, but lacked these traits of Duke. My senses took grasp of the feeling of that university and stay with me to this day.

It can be unexplainable at times the way forks in the road of life can steer you in the direction of your subconscious. I have heard people explain this as karma, or something similar; if you want something bad enough the opportunities will appear before your eyes. I most certainly wasn't thinking of this at the time, at least not consciously.

It was a tremendous Christmas break in Connecticut, going back as a Division I college baseball player. I felt vindicated in my mind by those who had mocked me in the spring on wanting to play baseball in college. Their actions had given me the incentive to play harder than ever before. Coaches, former teammates, and the scouts all said otherwise, and wearing that Bulls logo on my jacket proved them wrong and now they knew about it.

Well, nothing of the sort transpired during my stay in the wintry elements of the New England state. I had many great times with friends and family over Christmas and received some congratulatory remarks on making the team. Baseball wasn't even an afterthought.

I really hadn't accomplished much in the grand scheme of things. I could fall flat on my face in my first appearance and never get another chance. An injury during the season without having a scholarship and I would be cast off as a never-was. This was a chance to get to the next level. Pitching for the Bulls, a player the coaches consider to be an important part of the team. This would require even more determination, perseverance, and luck to be given this opportunity then putting myself in the position to receive it.

Traveling back to Tampa after the break, there was plenty of time to think. I asked myself, "What it would take over the next month before games start in order to get the chance to pitch?"

It'd be one month before our first game when classes started. This semester would be more challenging in terms of classes, so getting a head start keeping up with them would be crucial. Wilton High School was as good as any college preparatory school in Fairfield County, Connecticut, in spite of being a public institution.

I've always felt that my education there was exceptional because of the level of faculty and peers. Virtually every senior student enrolled in college and the curriculum was college prep as well. However, poor discipline and study habits caused struggles with the college curriculum at USF.

I graduated middle of the pack in my class. Ranked 182 of 365 students put me at 50%, and I felt satisfied because of the caliber of the students in the class. The classes at USF didn't seem that much harder in terms of the material, but the speed at which we were expected to learn was greater.

The biggest problem was the anticipation of the season starting and trying to focus on the classes. It was becoming apparent that I would make the traveling team. This was another realized goal before the spring, and this would mean consideration as one of the pitchers to be counted on to contribute. Our first game would be in Miami, a four-team round robin tournament called "The Florida Four." Florida State, Florida, and South Florida would join Miami at the famed Mark Light Stadium in downtown Coral Gables in the first week of February.

What a start! My first college baseball games were against two of the best college teams, Florida State and Miami. Miami had just won the College World Series in Omaha, Nebraska two years prior, and their team was stacked with future professional players. Florida State was almost as good, with a bunch of future pros of their own. Florida, though not as good, still had quality players themselves. The coach for Miami, Ron Fraser, was a living legend, and he and FSU's Mike Martin were considered two of the best Division I coaches in the country.

Thinking about the upcoming tournament, I'd find myself daydreaming in class. Once in a while, I would catch myself and try to be disciplined about focusing on the task at hand, but to no avail. I was hooked on the euphoria of what was to come. Thank goodness that day finally came, and we were on our way to Miami!

What I remember the most about that entire tournament was the absolute joy of arriving at the Airport Marriott on Lejeune Ave. in Miami. After getting our itinerary shortly before arrival, we waited for our room assignments and shuffled off to our new homes for the next three nights.

"This is not real," I said to my roommate.

Staying at the Marriott and playing baseball against the best teams in the NCAA? Less than a year before not even considered one of the best players on my high school team, or one of the best three pitchers, and now this? I walked into the room and literally jumped on the bed like a five-year-old kid about to go to Disney World for the first time!

My enthusiasm and excitement of the moment were unabashed and I just let loose. After 30 seconds or so, not wanting to injure myself or explain to the coaches about breaking a bone while jumping on the bed, I finally calmed down and rested.

The next day the team went to the stadium for our first game against none other than Florida State. We ended up losing to FSU by one run that day against one of the two teams I had hoped to play for. To participate that weekend in Miami was more exciting than anything personally experienced to that point. Florida State would play us again in Tampa the following weekend and beat the Bulls in three consecutive games, so four of the first five losses for the Bulls would be against FSU. It was fun to watch the team from Tallahassee as they just had a different way of playing the game. They always put pressure on you by running and bunting, and defensively they were amongst the best in college baseball.

As the spring season wore on in the first month, there was little chance to warm up in the bullpen. Game after game went by and the thought of getting an opportunity to pitch became a growing source of anxiety. Even worse was alienating myself from the other teammates by doing something that is considered sacrilegious in the clubhouse.

Our team was making many defensive errors, and we had lost a few games because of it. In fact, we hadn't had a game that was error free all year going into our tenth game, so the team decided all players couldn't shave until we finished a game without an error.

This was the way to break the curse, so going along with the team was not optional. Does it matter if you prefer to be clean shaven all the time? No, deal with it until the curse has been lifted no matter what!

Baseball is a game played by men with a great many superstitions. When something is decreed sacred, no matter the circumstance, the decree needs to be respected. My experience was limited to this point and I didn't know the ramifications of this unwritten rule between teammates. Not feeling like a part of the team and angry to have to deal with this situation caused errors in my judgment. My reasoning was plausible. I had no playing time to this point, so why deal with their problems? We eventually will go a game without an error, right?

The next four games go by, and we can't get through five innings without somebody making an error of some kind. Then came the poor decision which is still most regrettable to this day, "I don't give two craps about this stupid self-imposed shaving strike because I have nothing to do with it."

When I arrived in the clubhouse the next day with my freshly shaven face, it was like committing a mortal sin. I was convicted by the "Kangaroo Court" immediately! When the team does something like that, it means "team." It didn't matter that I came from an unknown town in Connecticut that had no tradition or understanding of superstitions that violate team imposed sanctions such as this. It was a lesson indoctrinated by the rest of the team regarding chemistry.

After being verbally abused by the entire team for two days, the padlock for my locker was wound up with masking tape and somebody used a Sharpie and made little dots that represented whiskers on a face. That was it; I was ready to quit and leave the team after that! This one, little, stupid thing I had unfortunately done had put me to the point of quitting.

Ken Ericksen finally came to my aid and told me by putting myself ahead of the team regardless of the circumstances was wrong, and players who don't respect this will be severely frowned upon. He told me eventually everybody gets a shot; be a stand-up guy and take the abuse by the team and it would be accepted.

He was correct, and after taking the medicine for a few more days, it was over. Finally, in Tallahassee against Florida A&M, we broke through without an error, and the shaving strike was over. Fittingly, a player who had many errors during the streak picked up a groundball with two outs in the ninth.

Ralph Gali looked at the dugout with a huge smile and said, "It's over!" as he threw to first. He was as relieved as anybody on the team.

I'd learned my lesson not to go against any team sanctioned activity no matter how trivial. In baseball, to be considered an individual means you put yourself ahead of the team.

Soon after this, the reality of getting a chance to play was imminent. We were 9-6, the pitching staff was pretty ordinary and depleted, and so the perception was that the team needed more depth. Some of the guys were starting to tire and get sore arms. This was my chance to get an appearance within the next few games. Then, on March 2, 1984, that chance would finally come.

6 VALIDATION

That evening, a surprise was waiting for me at the baseball game: Ed Moore showed up out of nowhere to visit me. His older sister was attending USF and he had some time to kill before an evening function. I told Ed to hang around because this was going to be the day for an opportunity to pitch. Understandably, Ed had an invite to a sorority function and the implications of that far exceeded any desire to watch the game. Who could blame him? He was down from Furman on spring break and his parents lived in Tampa. So after a brief five minute exchange, he was off to his party, and I was back in the dugout again waiting for my first opportunity to play.

We were playing Stetson University and they had always fielded a decent team. Sure enough, toward the end of the game with us up by a run, Coach Roberts told me to go warm up in the pen. Jumping up as soon as my name was called, I was already headed down there before he even finished his sentence.

After getting loose, Ron Cardieri came down and said I had the seventh inning, maybe the eighth. Reaching the mound for the first time, yet another accomplishment was made. Now I didn't hold anything back and competed like never before. The ball left my hand with velocity I had never had previously.

As the ball hit the glove the exclamation by Scott Hemond was, "Whewee!! Spike's got it going tonight!"

Everybody who plays baseball in college and the pros has a nickname, without fail. It's one of the more peculiar things about this sport.

Ken Ericksen asked me one day at practice about the scar over my lip, I told him of the time when I was 13, playing in the backyard with my friends. We had our own "Olympics," and one of the events was the "railroad spike throwing event." Well, now that the hair has come down off the back of your neck, nearly the worst outcome happened. As I came out from behind the garage my friend had thrown the spike, and it hit me square in the upper lip. The damage to my mouth required plastic surgery. Instantly, Ken anointed me with the nickname "Spike," and it will be forever associated with players I played with at USF.

Scotty's verbal acceptance really fired me up as the first batter stepped up to the plate. Remembering how that inning went is foggy to this day. No hits or runs and struck out one, but it is still all a blur. The eighth went well and again, I finished unscathed. Jerry Comellas then came in to get the save, and we won 4-2.

What a great first appearance and night that was. The feeling of contributing to the team was great, and now I wanted to prove even more to be an asset for the rest of the season. Well, not knowing when the next chance would be—we enjoyed the moment. The University of Miami was coming in that weekend and the probability to even warm up was unlikely. The

Hurricanes were one of the best teams in the country. The ice was broken, and the next opportunity to play would come sooner than later.

The Bulls really started playing well and played toe to toe against the Hurricanes in the weekend series. After taking the first two games the thought of sweeping the team that won the CWS just two short years ago wasn't only in sight, but expected in the minds of the players. The fielding problems the players were having earlier in the season had been eliminated. The pitching was starting to come into rhythm and our hitters were in a zone.

Going into the final game, we felt great about our chances and that our hitting barrage wouldn't let up. Fortunately for us, it didn't, because Miami wasn't letting up that day and they were hitting the ball well. Then in the seventh inning with us up by a couple of runs, Coach Roberts told me to start warming up.

Unbelievable! This was UM, one of the best teams in the NCAA. I was going to pitch against them. Our starter was struggling, so I was called to come in and save the day for the Bulls. Just like the last outing, Scotty was there to fire me up, and it worked. The first hitter was Doug Shields, a player from the Tampa area who'd made a big impact during the championship year they had in 1982.

I remembered him from the tournament in Miami back during the Florida Four tournament. Any high-profile player I could do well against was icing on the cake. I'd love to punch this guy out, if given the chance. There were a couple of runners on and one out, so striking him out would be the best outcome possible.

After an arduous time at bat, Shields struck out on a slider and I thought, *Maybe this is the way it's supposed to be.* The next guy made an out to end the inning, and we scored a few more runs to put it out of reach. The USF fans were singing that famous song by Steam, "Na-Na-Na-Na, Hey-Hey-Hey, Goodbye!" while I pitched the last three innings to get the save.

That was the moment of validation for me about being good enough to pitch Division I baseball—pitching three hard innings and getting the save against Miami. The next week would be a trip to Tallahassee to play against Florida State!

In February, when we played Florida A&M, we didn't get the chance to visit the Florida State campus. I was certainly excited to do so. Every time we stepped on a campus for the first time was thrilling to me, but going to Tallahassee this time was extra special. As we approached FSU, seeing those old style buildings and landscape similar to Duke just months before made for a perfect night.

When we arrived at the baseball field, it had more personality than any other venue I had played in up to that date. The stadium looked perfect; the entire wall that surrounded the field was lined with tall pine trees, and it was situated right next to the football stadium. This was going to be a fun place to play!

The short right field fence had given FSU's Jeff Ledbetter the home run record in the NCAA just a few years ago looked so easy to put the ball out. Then came the fans, wow!

They were considered some of the most brutal to deal with in the country. Mark Rose, who happened to be rooming with both Ken and me, was going to start the first game of the series and had some advice for me.

"If you get out there to pitch, these are absolutely necessary," Rose said.

He then handed me two cotton balls to put in my ears! Well, Mark was right...the most noise came from the area known as "Section B, Home of the Animals." Section B was led by someone known as "Mongo." Steven Budnick was the guy who would raise his hands in the air to incite the section to start yelling. Then all of a sudden he would throw his hands to make the letters: N-O-L-E-S, and everyone would scream "NOLES!"

Absolutely crazy!

Another crazy chant they'd do would occur when a coach would come out to visit the pitcher that was in the game. These dugouts had five steps down into the sunken area that was below the level of the field. If you weren't used to them, they could be a hazard. Well, the Section B fans would chant, "Hut, Hut, Hut, Hut!"

This would continue until the coach reached the pitcher's mound, and they did the same on the way back. The only thing different was on the way back, what they'd say upon arrival to the steps was, "Trip, stumble, fall, boom, into the dugout!"

These guys were hilarious!

Although they could be downright brutal on the opposing players during the game, they also gave equal time to players who made a great play. Upon arriving into the dugout, an opposing player who made a great play was given a standing ovation by Section B and was most certainly respected. We ended up losing two of three games in the series that weekend against the Seminoles, but it was the most enjoyable of the trips we had made so far that year.

The rest of the spring went well with more opportunity to play. Soon, Coach Roberts gave me a starting role on the team. Although there were some poor outings, I managed a 2-1 record in 1984 with an earned run average just over four. Our season ended against South Alabama in the Sunbelt Conference Tournament in Mobile as the Jaguars beat us 3-2 in a hard-fought game.

I pitched just shy of 40 innings my freshman season, and the majority of the runs attributed to my ERA were from a poor outing against Harvard. All in all, a successful year with the prospects of coming back next year in line as a starting pitcher. The experience pitching against some of the best teams in the NCAA could be useful for any summer league team.

The spring of 1984 was the pinnacle for me for baseball to that point. Realizing some of the dreams and goals were fulfilling, to say the least. I was drained from all the activity—and believe it or not, the stress associated with playing at USF. The love for playing was always there, but looking over your shoulder and hoping they didn't call you into the office and say "get lost" was ever too present. The memory of getting kicked off the JV high school team as a junior was always in the back of my mind. Knowing that I would play ball over the summer without that stress was a bit liberating.

After the season and classes were over, I packed my things and made arrangements to stay with my grandparents in Norwalk, Connecticut for the summer. It was exciting to think about spending the summer in Connecticut with friends and play baseball with two teams, the Wilton Reds and the American Legion team in Fairfield.

Unlike college, just because you were a pitcher didn't preclude you from other positions. Almost all college pitchers never played or hit once they were drafted or recruited as a pitcher. The summer in 1984 was relaxing, fun, and very helpful in recharging my batteries for the upcoming fall season with USF. One thing I remember most fondly was arriving in Norwalk that summer.

Some high school friends of mine from Wilton were meeting for dinner that night, and I was really looking forward to being there. The more important item on the list that day was to secure employment before heading to dinner. Arriving in Norwalk around two, I set out and had a job before five. The local Wendy's hired me on the spot, and I had a blast working as the grill man for the lunch shift.

My grandmother was so impressed with what was a completely innocuous event that for the next 30 years, she told people how I got a job for the summer in one hour! I always smiled every time she told that story during family get togethers.

The fall of 1984 came quickly, and I was prepared for making my mark on the starting rotation at USF. Many of the USF players believed I had showed enough promise as a freshman to be a lock for the rotation.

There were many things about this fall that were completely different—no tryouts, familiarity, and a place on the team. Fellow players were telling me that I had the chance to be a starter for the next three years and could do exceptional things. There were many things to look forward to this fall and by continuing to work hard and show enthusiasm they would come to fruition.

The fall season was much like the previous season with many scrimmages and games against JUCO teams in Florida. When we traveled down to Palm Beach to play Palm Beach Community College, my roommate and I ended up getting left behind at the restaurant after the game.

Before the bus would leave the coaches would always say, "Check for your roomie."

This would make sure everybody was on the bus, and nobody got left behind. Well, my roomie for the trip was Rob Nickel, and we were in the bathroom when the bus decided to leave. Rob remarked as we realized the error of the checking system, "Yeah, great system."

Well, Eddie Cardieri happened to drive his own vehicle to Palm Beach and was with Scott Hemond and Mark Rose. They saw that we were left behind.

"Get a taxi to the bus station and find your way back to Tampa," Cardieri said as Mark and Scott laughed while they drove off.

It would have been a tight fit in Eddie's vehicle, but I still feel a bit slighted about him not helping us get back to Tampa that day. This incident would play a factor later in the spring of 1985 during the season.

A new season as an experienced college player brought a different feeling going into the fall. The teams we played in the fall were predominantly younger players. It was problematic to get these guys and could prove costly. Miami, Stetson, and South Alabama were all good NCAA teams, but the fall wiped the slate clean. You needed to prove once again that you belonged on the team.

Baseball is such a cognitive game for the player. Most players think way too much. If we could control the thinking process having to do with off-field items, we would be less neurotic. Ultimately, we needed to be robotic and not think about the things we can't control. The fall season ended with no great fanfare, and I was in the position to make a contribution to the team on the pitching staff.

USF had brought in a number of new players and pitchers. This made it difficult for me to overtake some of the scholarship players for pitching time. There were seven new pitchers—all on scholarship of some sort—which did not bode well for me. I was about to get an education about politics and opportunity when it comes to NCAA baseball. Being cast in the same role as the previous year (spot starter and middle to long relief) was pleasing; it guaranteed a role on the team.

The spring season started with great hope for the USF team, but those hopes were dashed swiftly. We started up against Miami and then played Florida State in Tallahassee, losing all three games. Then we lost to crosstown Division II University of Tampa before heading to New Orleans for a tournament during Mardi Gras.

The team was in a bit of disarray when Coach Roberts called for a team meeting before our trip. We were nearly winless over the first couple of weeks after being ranked number 19 in the country by *Collegiate Baseball*. After our 1-5 start, we wouldn't crack the top 25 the rest of the season.

Roberts was noticeably emotional as he spoke with us. He had made a decision about the team, but really didn't tell the players what was going on. The team found out that he decided this would be his last year coaching the Bulls, and a successor would need to be named. He was most emotional about Scott Hemond—by far the best player recruited during his tenure, and that he wouldn't be there during Scott's last season at USF.

The trip to New Orleans was by far more entertaining off the field than on. On our 12-hour bus trip from Tampa, we arrived on Friday during Mardi Gras. As we exited the bus, some of the locals were getting sick in the street.

"Welcome to New Orleans!" Cardieri exclaimed.

We entered the Clarion Hotel on Canal Street near the center of the action. New Orleans was certainly an eye-opener when it came to a reality check about life. Being 19 years old on Bourbon Street during Mardi Gras isn't your normal situation for any college sophomore. I sure did like all the little hot dog stands that were turned into Hurricane stands serving well past midnight!

Bourbon Street is known for many things: strip clubs, drinking, and nightlife surrounded us as the parade of beads commenced. Walking with a group of college baseball players down that street would most assuredly require entry of a few of the local establishments.

What was interesting about these clubs was that many of the "entertainers" were actually college students working their way through college! That weekend was educational as much as anything else I learned during my college years.

We also played baseball over the weekend. It was a round robin with two other teams, University of New Orleans and Wichita State. Each team would play the other twice during the weekend. Unfortunately, USF would only win one game and tensions would remain high. I did get an appearance, my first of the season, against Wichita State. I gave up one hit and then induced Dan Raley, their All-American second baseman, to hit into a double play to end the inning.

After the last game, we were headed back to Tampa with a 2-9 record and no answers for the future. The coaches seemed unsure, and after Roberts's emotional speech, the players were unsure of the future as well. *Don't think about anything, just do your best by focusing on pitching well on the next opportunity.*

My next appearance would come against Florida a few days later where I pitched and not particularly well, giving up a couple of runs in an inning. Although it wasn't a good outing, little did I know it would be my last official appearance ever at USF.

That weekend we had a chance to host Oklahoma State University in Tampa for their opening baseball series for 1985. The Cowboys were one of the best teams in college baseball in 1985 and had two outstanding players on the team, Pete Incaviglia and Doug Dascenzo.

Watching Incaviglia hit the ball during batting practice was nothing less than astounding as the pitching staff watched him crush ball after ball 100 feet over the fence.

"Don't be intimidated by that, boys. I've given up a few of those in my time!" Roberts proclaimed.

Roberts retired with the Phillies, giving up more home runs

than any other pitcher in baseball history, so he spoke from experience! Well, the slugger didn't disappoint. The first at bat he had that season was an 88 mph fastball by the starter Marty Valentine that went out of the yard quicker than it was pitched. Incaviglia went on to hit 48 home runs that year to set a NCAA record for home runs hit in one season.

Oklahoma State went on to the College World Series (CWS) that year, losing their last game to the eventual NCAA Champions University of Miami, as Greg "Hurricane" Ellena had one of the most prolific CWS tournaments ever in 1985 for UM.

Less than a week went by when a scheduled scrimmage game between USF and the Chicago White Sox would happen at their spring training home in Sarasota. The skipper for the White Sox was former USF student and Alum Tony LaRussa. The White Sox also had infielder and former USF player Tim Hulett. More than anything the game was arranged as a thank you to Coach Roberts and supposed to be a friendly match for the college kids to have fun.

The most exciting element of this game was to see one of the White Sox pitchers that was recently signed, Tom Seaver.

Seaver was my hero growing up in southern Connecticut. The future Hall of Famer was the one pitcher that many kids tried to model themselves after while growing up. Not approaching him on the field and letting him know what his career did for me was regrettable. At least I was on the same field with him for one game in my life.

It was apparent that our pitching staff was not ready for a MLB team as the White Sox made us look pretty bad. The players after the game said that it's not that our pitchers were bad, it's just we only threw two pitches, and in MLB, you need more than that. In fact, the only pitcher who did well was a little lefty named Brian Osgood who mixed in a change along with his fastball and curve.

Brian was a senior engineering major who was a little more "left-handed" than your typical lefty. Baseball players have always found left-handed pitchers a little off, so to speak, and Brian certainly hit that mark. One day we were playing University of Alabama-Birmingham in Tampa and we were in the bullpen goofing off watching the game. One of the players for UAB was future MLB player Hector Villanueva, who played for the Chicago Cubs from 1990-1993. Well, Hector was not the skinniest of guys, so Brian decided to have some fun at Hector's expense.

Brian walked down to the Sun Dome to make a phone call, as there were no cell phones back then, to Domino's Pizza and ordered five pepperoni pizzas to be delivered to Hector. Sure enough, two innings later, the Domino's delivery guy shows up with five fresh, hot, pepperoni pizzas looking for him in the visitors' dugout.

Both teams were laughing hysterically as the pizza guy was trying to deliver the goods. If you've ever watched an MLB game and have seen the pitchers in the bullpen and wondered what they do and talk about—this was a good example of what comes from it.

Well, I came in to pitch after Brian and contributed to the carnage, giving up a number of hits. What was worse was accidentally hitting the former USF player Hulett on the wrist. After hitting the USF alum, I received a look that was more on the side of aggravation than disgust by Hulett. Although not pleased by the outing, this was a scrimmage. It wasn't going to affect our position on the team, so I could just learn and grow from the experience. That wasn't the case from the coaches' point of view.

After the game, Roberts approached me and expressed his displeasure for my outing. I felt my heart sinking as he continued to tell me that he had reservations about the rest of the season for me and that I needed to work on some things before seeing the mound again. I said nothing to defend myself. He was a Hall of Fame baseball player and deserved respect, regardless of whether I agreed or not. That fork in the road was once again approaching, and a decision would possibly be on the horizon.

With all the dramatics, it was still exciting to face Florida State again that weekend. We played them well without much success over the past two years, and maybe we could win a series against them this year. That Saturday morning it was overcast with the threat of rain, and an overall dreary day that would only get worse. Nobody was sure that the game would happen as rain clouds constantly threatened during the pregame workouts that morning.

About an hour before the game, I was called over to speak with Coach Roberts. He delivered the news that hit me like the thunderbolt everybody there was expecting from the sky due to the weather.

He told me that they were going to exercise a redshirt and I would come back next year as a sophomore with three years of eligibility still remaining to play baseball. A redshirt in college athletics is a player who participates in practice but is not considered on the active roster. An NCAA athlete can play a maximum of four years and is given five years to complete their eligibility. This means I would still have three years left of eligibility.

What he was telling me seemed unbelievable after all the hard work and sacrifice. What had I done that year to have them consider a redshirt season? I hadn't even been given a chance to play this year and was now cast off for future years. This didn't make any sense.

It wasn't as if any of the other pitchers were playing well and our record was affected by my poor play. It must have had something to do with me accidentally hitting Hulett in the game against the White Sox. Whatever the reason, my actions over the next two days were to proactively seek a better opportunity. After undressing my USF uniform for the last time, I went back to the field where I found Ken Ericksen in the stands to help me through this difficult circumstance.

He was in school earning his master's degree and came to watch the Seminoles play the Bulls. Speaking with Ken gave me further insight to the events happening around me, and possible reasons for them. He said to me that sometimes we don't understand why things happen, but they do. Ken said he didn't agree with the decision Coach Roberts made, but it was still his decision. No matter what my thoughts were, it wouldn't change. I told Ken the decision was unacceptable and on Monday, the transfer paperwork to another school would be filled out.

The Bulls ended up splitting that weekend with the Seminoles and FSU won the first game of the series on that fateful day. On Monday following I entered the USF Athletic building and spoke with Jeff Davis, the Associate Athletic Director for USF. I asked for a transfer.

Unaware of needing permission due to the rules regarding players from Division I transferring to other Division I schools, I later realized that being a walk-on meant transferring without permission. Mr. Davis said that although he'd like to see me stay, he understood my position and wished me well wherever I ended up. That was that. I didn't go to any games or practices and tried to concentrate on getting my grades good enough to transfer to a school that turned me down as a senior in high school, Florida State University.

Later that spring, Robin Roberts publically announced that he'd be stepping down and retiring at the end of the season. It was rumored that Eddie Cardieri would most likely be given the opportunity to be head coach, and he did earn it.

Playing for Eddie was fun. The players liked him. They believed he would do a good job. For me, the situation at USF wouldn't change much, so transferring would be best. I also remember that night in Palm Beach that Rob and I were left and didn't get back to Tampa until after 5:00 a.m. I still hadn't gotten over it. Although the person who sent me packing was gone, I still felt I needed to transfer.

The four longest months of my baseball career were between March and July of 1985. The taste of Division I was still there, especially since I succeeded and was later abandoned for little reason by a Hall of Fame coach who never told me why. The keys to success were in my hands after my freshman year, but I was never allowed to use them to open any locks to my future.

I had performed well against worthy opponents. They needed to be used as the stepping stone for opportunity elsewhere. I decided to go for my dream shot, playing at Florida State. I mean, why not? I was able to overcome the obstacles of playing for a small school in Connecticut and walking on to a Division I school. Now, with a resume of pitching and getting a save against a Division I school that recently won the College World Series, I was sure FSU would welcome a pitcher with those credentials.

As I spoke with my parents about my decision about where to transfer to, my father had reservations regarding FSU.

"Why not University of Florida?" my father protested. "They have a good program with history."

Fact was, my father liked me being near home in Tampa, and Tallahassee was twice the distance away. Playing at Florida State had been my dream since I was in Little League, and attempting to play there and failing would make me happier than any other result.

I know in my heart that I tried for my dreams and wherever the chips fell, I'd accept them. Soon after in the middle of June, I made the call to Mike Martin, head coach at Florida State.

"Son, don't tell me your name. What you need to do is apply to FSU and once you're accepted, contact the baseball office," Martin said.

He was afraid of all the rules regarding the recruitment of athletes. Even though I was hardly an athlete worthy of recruitment, it could still be construed as tampering to some people.

That day I had everything in order to apply to FSU and sent the application off. This application included an essay in which I explained my desire to play at FSU since childhood. It might be needed as my GPA was barely a 2.5 at the time. In July, my acceptance to FSU arrived in the mail, and it was time to make preparations for the next phase of my life.

All of a sudden there was new hope and opportunity with baseball. I called Mike Martin back and told him of my acceptance and wanted a tryout with the team during the fall that year. He agreed that my experience playing against Miami, Wichita State, and Florida earned me a chance to tryout with the team, and I was given a two-week trial period. This was fine by me! In the fall, I would wear a Florida State baseball jersey and compete against the same players from that spring. The chance to make the spring team was in sight and now it was time to prepare.

There was a reason to believe in myself again. April and May were the worst, running and throwing every other day alone against a wall in a nearby park, and now a chance to play at FSU. I told my parents of what I accomplished through my efforts, and they were happy to see my opportunity to continue playing and competing at the highest level in college baseball.

I ended up finding a team to pitch with over the summer called the Tampa Smokers, and it was managed by former USF Bull, Ray Retinellar. One day in June while pitching at USF for the Smokers, Eddie Cardieri showed up. He was announced as head coach for the Bulls and was hoping to get me back on board.

He explained to me that the decision to cut me in the spring wasn't his and wanted me to return to USF and be the number three starter next spring. They had a great team coming back, the recruiting class was good, and he wanted me to be a part of a new atmosphere in Tampa. I let Eddie know about the transfer to Florida State and that there was no changing direction at this point. Truth was, all the paperwork was signed and going back was impossible. Even if it was possible, the answer would've been no.

Remembering what happened in Palm Beach still left a bad taste in my mouth. Eddie was just trying to keep me from going to a rival school. Things are different now between us, and those negative feelings have long since subsided. Eddie remained the head coach until 2006. Many critics said he should've done better, but the Bulls have regressed since his departure. Eddie left the field that day believing I'd most certainly come back, but I didn't believe it was going to haunt him.

7 GOING FOR THE DREAM

As the summer season for the Smokers came to an end, we had the chance to go to Wichita, KA and play in the National Baseball Congress (NBC) World Series. Our team played two games and lost both. It was an awfully long way to drive to just play two and go home, but we had fun anyway. Now it was time to pack my bags and head up to Tallahassee.

The excitement that ran through my veins was more than anything that could possibly be drug-induced. The very thought of putting on the uniform for the first time and running on the field as a Seminole was no longer a thought but a reality. Even if it was only for two weeks, I continued to tell myself to understand that my next goal was to be there for three weeks, then four and so on. Every small goal that was accomplished led to the larger one—making the team.

As my father and I drove up, there were many thoughts about that summer working for him at the Cadillac dealership in

Clearwater. He'd gotten the position there as the service manager when the job he originally had with another dealership was retracted in the summer of 1983. Because of the situation, my parents struggled to make ends meet, and I knew me being in college made things worse.

Each week during the summer, I would give Dad my paycheck and tell him to put it away for me while I kept $20 for myself. It was a fun job, parking lot boy. We would get the sold vehicles ready for delivery, occasionally pick up a customer who was getting work done on their car, move cars around the lot, etc. I quickly developed a friendship with the other lot boy, Tom Tivador.

Tom was a short, somewhat stocky individual who looked like the comic Gallagher. Simply one of the funniest individuals I was lucky to know. Tom was put on this earth to do just one thing, make other people laugh! Well, that summer we had a lot of fun, usually playing pool at one of the local places in and around Clearwater.

One particular evening we were to meet up at a place called "Flamingo Road" just south of SR 60 on US 19. I happened to get there early and ordered a beer. The College World Series championship game was on ESPN, and the game was in the last inning.

I had forgotten that the series was almost finished, being busy at work and waiting for my acceptance letter from Florida State that I'd sent in earlier that month. I watched in awe as Ric Raether from Miami—a submarine pitcher with a devastating slider against right-handed hitters—was dealing against Texas. Miami was up 10-6 and was about to win their second national championship in four years.

Without saying a word, I had thought to myself while watching Raether pitch at that moment, "Lord, it'd be a dream come true if I could pitch the last inning of the College World Series. I don't know what I could do to repay a dream like that, but all I know is that it would be the most amazing dream come true if that could happen."

As I watched Raether finish off the Longhorns, the Hurricane players started jumping on a human pile in the middle of the infield and I felt the emotion of the moment. After the moment, I turned away from the TV because in my heart that was just a dream and not reality. I couldn't fathom being in that position, and at the moment I was a player without a team. Would FSU give me the possibility of realizing goals and dreams? The rest of my future would be unveiled over the next month.

I didn't realize that my dad was trying to talk with me while daydreaming about watching the CWS back in June. We were getting close to Tallahassee and going to spend whatever time was left visiting the campus. Osceola Hall was an off-campus dorm near the west side of campus and would be my new home. My girlfriend at the time knew a friend that was staying there and suggested we room together if possible.

Elise and I met at USF and had been dating for over a year. When I decided to transfer, she did as well. Her friend Jim was involved with the FSU Circus. FSU is the only university in the country that has a circus, and Jim was one of the trapeze performers. We finally arrived and moved my belongings into the first-floor dorm room and quickly went off to visit the campus. My father got a hotel room for the evening and left the next morning. He was really impressed with the campus and instantly became a Seminole fan. He stayed that way until passing away in 2010.

After Dad left for Tampa, it wasn't long before I started preparing for classes and tryouts. Because I wasn't on the baseball team, I didn't get any preferential treatment when it came to classes. Unfortunately, I would have to sit in drop/add to get classes that didn't conflict with the afternoon baseball practices.

This was a little presumptuous of me, but I didn't come all this way to fail. Any college grad will tell you of the nightmare you deal with going through drop/add, because you could wait in line for hours only to have the last spot in a class taken by the person in front of you. Most of the day all you did was two things, sweat and pray. In the August heat, you were usually sweating more than praying!

After about four hours my schedule was completed and I could start concentrating on getting ready for the tryout. The first practice wouldn't be for a week because they were holding open tryouts for student walk-ons the first four days.

Dealing with the walk-on tryouts in Tampa at USF was downright grueling, and I wanted no part of that deal. Being able to avoid the open tryout gave me a better chance to eventually make the spring team and thankfully, Coach Martin agreed. It ended up after the walk-on tryout a few players were invited to participate for fall practice. This didn't earn them a spot on the spring team, but they would need extra guys to scrimmage over the fall, so it worked well.

One of those players was sophomore outfielder Greg Clayborne from Jacksonville's Ed White High School. This tall, lanky kid had a monster arm and hit home runs during the tryout from both sides of the plate. There were a few others, mostly pitchers, that didn't impress me, but I knew that they needed them for the fall.

The first day of practice started with a quick meeting with all the players that returned from the 1985 team, and the new recruits and invited walk-on players such as myself. Altogether, there were around 40 players. Coach Martin gave us a rundown of how the next few weeks would go. Because the field on campus was being worked on, most of the activities would be on the baseball field for the local high school, Florida High.

Florida High was literally on the campus for Florida State and had many programs for prospective teachers graduating from the University. Most of what we would be doing over the next few weeks would be evaluating talent. The coaches would also decide what players would make the fall competing squad against the JUCO teams that came in during the fall season. Once they determined this, they would make final determinations through a number of factors that included attrition(losing players to grades or injury), hustle, talent, and performance.

That was it. Players had two to three weeks to prove their worth, at least the ones who were not on scholarship. This situation was doable. I would not be out hustled, and I had already proved I could pitch against the teams FSU plays. Now I just needed to prove myself and get a little lucky.

Ever since high school, there hadn't been any coaches who believed in me and my potential as a pitcher. The first time I stepped onto a mound with Mike McLeod as my pitching coach was the day that all changed.

Mac was by far the most influential coach I ever had, and I owe him my success in the pitcher I became at Florida State. It didn't take him long to see flaws in my delivery that had set in over 10 years of repeated motion. My balance was off, my arm slot was inconsistent, and release point was all over the place.

"Ed, you're a pitcher with a real live arm and a screwed up delivery," Mac would say.

Unlike all the other coaches I'd encountered in my years of playing baseball, he was the first who wanted to try to realize my potential.

Most of those first two weeks Mac had me doing all sorts of

mechanical drills that would help in the areas I lacked, which was mostly balance. He said if we could fix my balance point, the rest would fall into place. It was also clear that he was spending a little more time with me than the others. This clued me in that I was going to be hanging on through at least the fall season. So, after two weeks went by and I still was on the fall team, it was apparent that I had passed the test.

We started up scrimmages in the third week at Florida High, and at times I was pitching against the heart of the Seminoles order. Luis Alicea, Paul Sorrento, Barry Blackwell, and Ed Fulton were all great hitters on the team this upcoming year. Pitching against them, I predominantly threw my best pitch—the slider—and they all had difficulty with it. Mac seemed pleased that my control had improved immensely due to the drills he put me through.

As the fall season games against the JUCOs started, I saw quite a lot of innings. I felt more and more a part of the team in some capacity. The spring team was still a long shot, but deep down, I just wanted to be a part of the team—even if it wasn't on the field. I'd gotten to know the players fairly well. We were like a fraternity that had parties and played cards. Although I had fun with some of the players at USF, this seemed much more of a tight-knit group. I felt more accepted here than at USF.

The fall season finally came to a close after about a 30-game schedule in which we lost four or five games. It was apparent that FSU had a strong team all the way around. Our infield had All-American Alicea at second, and potential All-American shortstop Bien Figueroa. Sorrento was another potential All-American in the outfield, and with returning players at first, third, and centerfield, this was a veteran lineup.

All that being said the strength of this team was on the pitching staff. Doug Little and Richie Lewis were consensus All-

Americans the past two years. Mike Loynd was poised to have a good year as the number two starter behind Little. Chris Pollack was a left-handed JUCO transfer from California with a plus fastball and a sweeping roundhouse curveball to finish the starting staff.

Also, we had Al Ashmont from New Jersey, a sophomore coming off some arm problems from last year, who was an All-American in high school. Al brought a 95 mph fastball to the plate. I'd never seen so many All-American players assembled on one field before! This was unreal! Also, newcomer Steve Kovensky from Palomar Junior College in California was one of the most sought-after pitchers in the country. Mike Lee from Chipola Junior College was yet another huge recruit for Florida State. FSU had the makings of what had to be the best staff in the USA. Paul Thomas was yet another tall lefty that would be counted on in relief, and I started to wonder, *How can I possibly break into this staff and get any playing time?*

Again, I had to tell myself that my goal is only one thing, to get a jersey. *When that time comes, and you realize that goal, we'll think about what's next.* Making the fall team and competing was validation enough in my mind that I belonged. It was the ability to believe you were good enough to play on the team that was the hardest part because some players with scholarships don't succeed. Very few walk-ons make the team and have virtually zero impact on a team of this caliber. Keep your goals on getting the jersey.

The winter break we had couldn't have gone any slower. The desire to start the spring season workouts consumed my mind. The focus was as sharp as it ever was, running and throwing occasionally to stay in shape to give myself the best chance to come out in January to compete for a spot on this roster.

Those weeks before spring workouts were crucial in my

preparation to make this team. I envisioned myself wearing the jersey and pitching at the beautiful stadium in Tallahassee. There needed to be this overwhelming feeling of just not accepting failure at this critical point, and nothing was going to distract the focus.

Then, some unfortunate luck started to help my future position with the Seminoles. Pitchers started getting hurt. Some were losing eligibility academically, and my stock was moving upward. I never wished any ill-will upon any of the pitchers on the team. It's bad karma and will bite you back if that's the way you roll.

It wasn't long before I realized that the pitching staff had basically lost three pitchers in some capacity. Al Ashmont, Mike Lee, and Paul Thomas were having elbow issues and would force the coaching staff to find alternatives. As the spring moved forward I continued to pitch, run, and work my ass off as hard as possible. Then, without any fan fair, I got my spot on the team as a relief pitcher. One of the best college baseball teams in the United States needed me in their bullpen and was happy to have me.

This was crazy! Less than three years earlier, I was cut from my junior varsity team and was now pitching for a top five Division I college team. Now that the jersey had been obtained, it was time to change goals, pitch once in a game for FSU! Remembering it took 17 games at USF to see my first action on the field gave me the strength to cope with the feelings of not getting into a game for a long period of time.

To be on the bench watching the game from a perspective of a small role player was more than I could've asked for three short years ago in high school. It was most certainly clear my role on the team would be limited. Some of the best and most highly recruited pitchers in the country were sitting next to me waiting to pitch as well. Still, the desire to pitch was real and the quicker I was able to get on the mound the better.

As the season approached, there was a competition heating up, but not the one you'd think of when it comes to baseball. There's a little-known tradition on the Seminole baseball team, and it's called the "Flag." It has been passed down to a new player on the team for many years.

The "Flag" is the American flag that flies directly behind the centerfield wall and is usually given from the player with the previous year's honor to a player of his choice the following year. The player receiving the flag is responsible for putting it up and taking it down during each home game. Needless to say, it's a dubious honor at best, so most new players stay on the good side of the previous honoree.

Keith Kidd was son of the Division II football coach Roy Kidd from Eastern Kentucky and had flag duties in 1985. One of the new players on this Seminole team was Deion Sanders, the legendary NFL cornerback in the Hall of Fame.

Well, Keith—coming from a football family—didn't take to Deion's hijinks and showboating on the gridiron very well. He let him know about it on more than one occasion. It was clear that Keith was going to give Deion the flag at the start of the season, whether he liked it or not. Keith practically taunted Deion about giving it to him, saying, "Deion, you'll accept the flag when I hand it to you, and you'll put that flag up!"

Deion would shout back, "I ain't putting up any flag you give me, Keith—I'm not doing it!"

This went on for a month right up to the first game, the day when the flag is officially handed to the next recipient. Keith would tell me I was lucky because if Deion wasn't on the team, I'd be doing the flag. Well, this was fortunate for me because I certainly didn't want to go back and forth every game!

The first game finally arrived, and as promised Keith held his ceremony and gave the flag to Deion. Reluctantly, Deion made the slow walk all the way around the field to put the flag on the pole and shimmied it up to the top. That was the happiest moment of the 1986 season for Keith, grinning from ear to ear watching Sanders do his duty with the Seminole tradition.

However, it would be short-lived for Kidd. Deion got injured shortly into the season rounding first base legging out a double and broke his ankle. This sidelined him basically for the rest of the season. When learning of the injury to the FSU star freshman football player, legendary head football coach Bobby Bowden decided that Sanders wouldn't play any more baseball games in 1986. He could participate in practice after his ankle healed with the approval of Bowden.

The more traditional baseball competitions were heating up as well with the starting pitching staff. Mike Loynd had overtaken Doug Little as the ace of the staff by being nearly unhittable during the spring. Conversely, Little had lost some velocity on his fastball, and his devastating slider was flattening out. This caused a lot of anxiety for the coaching staff as they expected Doug to have a huge year. Richie Lewis and newcomer Chris Pollack would fill out the rest of the staff, but were still undetermined where they stood behind Loynd.

The rest of the pitchers were Mike Lee, Steve Kovensky, Paul Thomas, Chris Dunn, and myself. Lee was considered the top closer with Kovensky in the setup role. Thomas was heavily recruited in 1984, but had not fared too well and had some injuries. Dunn, who was also a walk-on, and I were basically clean up role pitchers to prevent using the others in case of a blowout.

The pitching staff was set. Grambling would be our first opponent for 1986, and Florida State was expected to take all three games of the series. Grambling certainly wasn't a bad team that year, but not the caliber of FSU. Anything but an easy sweep would be considered disappointing.

There was a different feeling this team had compared to the USF teams from the previous two years. We were truly a team that had players and pitchers with specific roles—without the guesswork involved. My motivation was to do my very best to help my team win regardless of the amount of playing time received. Opportunities would be there with only nine pitchers, but how soon? Blowouts don't happen that often and the chance of playing in high leverage situations was miniscule.

That question was answered before the sunset that evening. Approaching the seventh inning and FSU up 9-0, McLeod told both Dunn and me to warm up in the bullpen. When he met us down there, he instructed us that Dunn would get the eighth and me the ninth.

And that was that. No waiting 17 games like the first year at USF. This was the most stressful inning I ever worked, and it was completed in about six minutes. When a player was put into a position that required no substitution other than excellence, stress will undoubtedly appear. Movies seem to make a mockery about stressful situations that require quick, accurate decisions. Over the years, I'd been fortunate to speak with young pitchers and players on the topic of stressful situations during a baseball game. Every time, it was always the same—two on or bases loaded, one out, you're up by a run, and their best hitter is at the plate. The fact is, only the person involved can define a stressful situation.

I took the mound and completed my warm-up pitches as the first batter approached the box. After receiving the ball from Barry Blackwell at third base, all I can remember from that point was this: *If I screw this up and don't get these guys out, I'll never see this pitcher's mound again.* The joy of my excitement to actually get on the mound the first game that season was quickly reduced in this highly stressful situation that only I was privy to! Instead of enjoying the moment, I wanted nothing more than to get off that field as soon as humanly possible! After all the problems at South Florida and now finally back on the field playing, I feared I might screw it all up! Where was the enjoyment?

It was crucial to get off the mound without problems because players not on a scholarship were expendable. Chris and I were thankful for the chance and happy to succeed. We also solidified ourselves in getting another opportunity down the road. "If you don't screw up, they'll always send you out again," I said to myself before each opportunity.

The journey was just as exciting as the arrival. In about six minutes or so, the three batters faced were retired, and I was able to breathe again. The game against Grambling that day in Tallahassee gave me the perspective about how even the most innocuous of game situations can be important.

After a few appearances, it was quite clear the coaches wanted to use me as a cleanup or "mop-up" man. After one of the starters finished six or seven innings, they'd hand me the ball to clean up. After about five appearances Mac came into the locker room before practice.

"You're starting against Richmond next Wednesday," Mac said.

I sat at my locker for about 15 minutes to take in the enormity of the situation that I'd be the fifth starter for a team with four All-American starting pitchers.

My determination had played a key role in getting to this point. Every time I approached the mound this fear of failing and never getting another chance was overwhelming. Starting was a whole new ball game. Just standing on the mound during the national anthem caused me to nearly hyperventilate!

The first inning was always the hardest for me. I tried to settle my nerves and succeeded by getting the first two hitters out. The third hitter smoked a ball to my left on the ground, and Alicea did a full layout dive and snagged the ball before it reached the outfield grass. He quickly rose and threw the runner out by a step. What an outstanding play! That play, I turned into a spectator and cheered like I was in the stands myself.

Because of that play by Alicea, I started getting into a groove and actually had a no-hitter after five innings. The sixth inning would prove to be my last as a couple of ground ball base hits, and a double chased me from the game. We won that game 12-4, and I earned my first win as a Seminole that evening. At this point, I gave myself a break and exhaled saying, "I think I can get away with a bad outing and still get another chance to pitch now."

This was about the time Deion broke his ankle and his baseball season came to an end. This news had a direct impact on me when Keith came up to me the next day and handed over the flag.

"At least you didn't have to put it up the entire season!" Kidd laughed.

I started the long walk around the stadium, happy to put the flag up. Believe it or not, this didn't bother me one bit. It was being part of this great team and how privileged I was to be there. Now that my position was solidified, the fun was starting to really set in. During the first part of the spring, FSU was nearly undefeated, going 33-5 through March and 48-8 through April. The coaches and players felt this was a good team, but to dominate all facets of the game made this one special. Great pitching, great defense, and great hitting for average were certainly the trademarks. Team speed was outstanding on defense and the base paths. The only way to beat this team was for us to make mistakes. About the only weakness, if there was one, was power. Paul Sorrento provided most of the home runs that year with 22. If the 1986 FSU baseball team played their "A" game, the other team didn't stand a chance.

Florida State's ranking in *Baseball America* and *Collegiate Baseball* had been in the top five virtually the entire year. By the time March rolled around, we were the top-ranked team in the NCAA. Every team we went up against gave us their best shot and we dropped them one by one without much struggle. The only time where we looked beatable was the first week in May during our three-game series in Miami, and the beginning of the Metro Conference Tournament in Tallahassee. As our regular season was coming to a close, we headed down to Miami for that important three-game series that would be another key opportunity for me to solidify my role on this team.

8 REALIZING THE DREAM

The series against Miami was especially important as both teams were trying to get one of the top seeds for the regionals that would be held in two weeks.

The game didn't start off well for our team as Miami seemed to have every hitter get on base. Before you knew it, they hit through the entire line up and scored eight runs and we had only made one out. By the time the last hitter approached the hitter's box, Coach Martin sent me to the pen to go warm up. Two hitters later, I was called in to pitch.

Martin sent me out to face Miami in what looked to be a concessionary move. It was 8-0 after one and I was to save the bullpen for the last two games.

As the game went on the FSU lineup started to chip away at the huge lead that the Hurricanes had as I continued to quiet their bats. Before you knew it, we had the lead in the eighth with a score of 10-9! The Canes were dumbfounded how they'd lost the lead, while I'd only given up two hits and a run through seven innings. Once regaining the lead, I started the ninth and gave up a leadoff single to Rick Richardi. I was pulled from the game and the Seminole fans who made the trip to Miami gave me a nice ovation.

Unfortunately for me, Miami came back with two runs in the ninth, and we ended up losing, 11-10. Although disappointed in the result, it was that game that proved I could be trusted in high leverage situations. Also, it was the first game that I decided to use ice because of all the throwing I did in 24 hours. I had a bullpen session with Coach Mac the evening before in which I threw at least 100 pitches.

After the game, I was instructed to speak with the Tallahassee radio station due to my performance that night. Walking up the bleachers at Mark Light Stadium to the press box, I happened to walk past the legendary coach for Miami Ron Fraser. He had just finished his interview with the radio press. As I walked by, he stopped me and said, "Eddie, I just wanted to let you know you really shoved it up our asses tonight!"

"Thanks, Coach!" I said.

I could feel the hair rising on the back of my neck as I entered the radio booth!

I don't even remember the interview I did after Coach Fraser's remark to me. I was in ecstasy by that point! Although disappointed that we lost the game I was happy in the effort we had battling it back.

That weekend series was the only series that year that Florida State baseball didn't take, as we split the last two games. The next week would be the Metro Conference tournament in Tallahassee. The staff would be fully rested to win the tournament and most importantly, a home regional. The conference tournament winning team gets an automatic bid to the regionals to qualify for the College World Series (CWS) in Omaha, Nebraska. Our motivation was to obtain a top seed ranking in Tallahassee making it easier to earn the right to go to Omaha. After a couple of tough games against South Carolina, we won the tournament and a top seed in Tallahassee was eminent.

The players knew we'd be very tough to beat at home with our crowd behind us. We had only lost three games in Tallahassee all year, so the confidence was high that we would return to Omaha for the first time in six years—if we could get the home regional as a top seed. Now that the regular season was over, we waited to see who was going to play us in the regional. It'd be at least 10 days before our first regional game, and that's enough time to make any baseball team rusty.

Florida State and Louisiana State were approached by ESPN to play a nationally televised game on May 19—three days before the regional opener. The national rankings had Florida State number one and Louisiana State number two in the polls, so they wanted to have the top two teams square off as a prelude to the College World Series later in the month. ESPN was the network that catapulted Division I college baseball to what it is today, with its innovative programming of "fringe sports" starting in the late seventies.

Both schools agreed, and our coaches decided to have each starter pitcher throw two innings each with Kovensky to throw the ninth. This would give our entire staff some work in a real game before the regional opener.

We were all pretty psyched as it was everybody's first televised game…well, all the starting pitchers, that is. Paul Thomas and I seemed to be the odd guys out because we had no chance of entering the game. Paul had been given some opportunities to pitch and was the next option after me in relief.

We talked the day before the game as I was driving with Paul in my car on campus.

"Man, here we are gonna play on ESPN, and we already know we're not going in, sucks big time!" Paul said.

I agreed, but knew my chances were much higher than Paul's.

Paul was the son of former MLB player Frank Thomas of the Washington Senators and was recruited by FSU in 1983 out of high school. Paul had a scholarship to play basketball at UNLV with legendary head coach Jerry Tarkanian, but turned it down to pitch and play first for FSU. He was a 6'6" right-handed pitcher who didn't throw particularly hard, but had a really good sinker. Paul struggled with arm problems, and it prevented him from having much success during his time in Tallahassee.

We had also found out who our opponents would be in our regional, Texas A&M, N.C. State, and University of South Florida. I couldn't believe it! We were going to play against the team I left last year for the right to go to Omaha, isn't that a kick in the head! We had played them four times over the season and lost only once, but USF had been in the top 20 all year long. Coach Cardieri was correct in his assessment of the USF team and how good they were going to be. It was going to be fun seeing my old teammates, and hopefully, we would end up victorious at the end of the tournament.

It was a cold, rainy Monday for the event, and there was a bit of a circus atmosphere surrounding the game. FSU and LSU were very similar teams. Great pitching and good defense with timely hitting were the trademarks of both teams. The Seminoles had the edge with team speed, and LSU had the edge at closing pitching with Barry Manuel. Manuel was 10-1 with eight saves that year and possessed one of the best fastballs in the country. If this game was close your chance of seeing him in the game hovered around 100%.

The Tigers also had one of the top players in the country, right fielder Joey Belle. Belle had 19 home runs to go with his .350 batting average that year. His surly attitude and demeanor towards opposing pitchers was well-documented and the intimidation he projected upon them was obvious. There were some other good hitters in the lineup, but the one you needed to focus on was Belle.

Conceding to the fact about not going in, it was time to settle in and watch a great game between these two teams. As the game went on, it didn't disappoint. It was nip and tuck through the eighth. The Noles held a 4-2 lead going into the top of the ninth. As Kovensky took the mound to end the game, Coach Mac told me to go warm up. It was clear that Steve wasn't comfortable being in this situation. He had not been faring well and had the tendency to give up home runs at the worst time.

The first hitter Kovensky faced was Mike Papajohn, the eighth hitter in the lineup. If his name sounds familiar, you're not mistaken. After his baseball playing days, he became an actor and had some familiar roles in movies, particularly Kevin Costner's *For Love of the Game*. He played the role of Sam Tuttle, the number three hitter and arch nemesis of Costner in the movie.

Well, Papajohn walked to bring up the catcher Craig Faulkner—a tall right-handed hitter that didn't hit for average, but could certainly hit for power. While warming up in the pen, Faulkner hit a ball that to this day, I'm not sure where it landed. In an instant, the score was tied at four, and it was apparent my role had just changed.

Kovensky continued to struggle. The leadoff hitter got an infield single, and then another single made it first and third with still nobody out. Worse than that, Joey Belle was stepping up to the plate. He had gone two-for-three with two doubles, one each against Doug Little and Richie Lewis. I'm sure Belle was licking his chops with the opportunity to hit against Steve, but he wouldn't get the chance. Martin was making his slow walk to the mound where he called for me to come in.

To say the least, that this was a surreal experience for me, was making it sound normal. A whirlwind of emotions were going through my head of all the problems I'd had with baseball throughout high school and USF. I wanted to think about all the coaches that didn't believe in my abilities. The problem was that this bad-ass named Joey Belle was approaching the box, and he was ready to take my head off.

The ESPN play-by-play guy Sam Rosen said it best that night as I approached the rubber to make my first pitch.

"I can't think of a worse situation for a pitcher to come into, two men on with nobody out, facing Joey Belle. Maybe the exception of there being the bases loaded," Rosen said.

I grabbed the ball from the catcher and toed the rubber ready to make my first pitch.

Belle had problems picking up the slider that I had thrown practically my entire baseball life. It's one of those pitches that, as a hitter, you see and wonder why you missed hitting it well. In my mind, striking out Belle was crucial, like cutting off the head of the snake. On a two and two pitch, I threw the best slider of my life and Belle missed the pitch that disappeared low and outside of the plate. Belle walked off the field, cussing at me about not throwing a fastball, then preceded to throw his bat and helmet in the dugout.

The next hitter walked, leaving the bases loaded. Feeling a good slider would get a double play, the next hitter swung at the first pitch and lifted a fly ball to short left field. The shortstop Bien Figueroa fielded the fly and kept the runner at third, two outs. Almost finished. I needed to get this last hitter out to keep the game tied at four.

Feeling confident, I started off throwing a fastball for a strike; then I induced the hitter to hit a slider that grounded into my glove for an easy play at first. Mission accomplished! I got us out of the inning without the guy on third scoring. The fans were roaring, and I'd been the hero of the night by taming the Tigers threat in the ninth. As much as I wanted to celebrate, I knew if we didn't score, I'd be back there for the tenth.

The bottom of the ninth proved to be correct for my earlier assumption. It was a close game, and we would see Barry Manuel for the Tigers. Barry's fastball would top-out in the mid-nineties, which was rare for a college pitcher in 1986. He had good control of the pitch and would generally induce weak swings for ground balls if he didn't punch you out.

Greg Clayborne was our first hitter, and he induced a walk to get our first runner on. After Alicea flew out to right field, Sorrento came up to the plate to face Manuel. Manuel's low fastball seemed to be right in the swing plane of Sorrento's upper-cut swing, so we hoped for a home run here. As Manuel's pitch came in Paul had a tremendous cut. Sorrento seemed to just miss the ball and fouled straight back behind home plate. He was right on target with the speed of the pitch.

This rattled the LSU Head Coach Skip Bertman, and he came out to speak with his catcher, which was ruled a visit from the dugout. I could only imagine he conveyed to him to tell Manuel not to throw that pitch in the same place again. Manuel apparently didn't listen—a carbon copy pitch came into Sorrento and it was the hardest ball I've ever seen hit in person. The ball went out of the park so fast you could barely keep up with it, and the game was over. The Seminoles defeated the Tigers 6-4 in a classic game for college baseball that year.

It was the coming-out party for me, and finally, I thought

about all the dreams I wanted for me as a college player. My laundry list of people I'd wanted to prove myself to was complete. Word would get around of the accomplishments from the game on ESPN. Classmates from Wilton had let me know of how they were just watching the game, and all of a sudden I was pitching in the game. The shock of it all completely freaked them out. What a great feeling that was. Still, there was more to do and the season for FSU was just starting.

Most college players start the season with a goal in mind. Individual goals and team goals are all part of any baseball player at all levels. For the Division I college player, it's simply one word, "Omaha." Omaha is the mecca of every college baseball player that has ever set foot on a diamond. It's to play for the "Sculptured Bat," the trophy given to the winning team in Division I each year. FSU was considered the front runner to win the title this year, and the regional was the first step to attaining the goal of winning the national championship.

We learned that our trip through the regional series would be a little easier as we were the top seed and given one with only four teams. In 1986, the regional bids were constructed differently than they are today. The number of qualifying teams in 1986 was 40 divided into four four-team and four six-team regional tournaments. Presently the field has been increased to a 64-team field through a series of 16 regional and eight super regional tournaments. The eight super regional winners face off in Omaha in the CWS.

Just to get to the regional series was the goal of most teams. It was hard enough to be one of the top 40 teams in Division I. We knew we would be in a regional shortly after the season started. Even losing the conference tournament wouldn't knock us out, so we felt that the beginning of our season started with the first regional game. Failing in this tournament would mean that our season would be considered a complete failure.

The opener was against the fourth-seed NC State, and after cruising to a 10-3 lead with Loynd on the mound, I finished the game throwing the last three innings. We had some difficulty in the ninth with a couple of bad hops, and the final score was 10-6—tough, but we got the job done.

The next game was the winner's bracket game. We faced Texas A&M who beat USF 10-2 in their opener. They were a good team with disciplined hitters and certainly a tough team to beat. At the end of the day, Florida State prevailed 12-9 in a hard fought hitting game. This put us as the only team without a loss after the first two days, and whoever came out of the loser's bracket would need to beat us twice, once against 19-1 Mike Loynd.

After USF beat Texas A&M the next day, the final would be FSU vs. USF for the right to go to the College World Series. Sometimes things just work out that make the storyline sound like fiction. Not that this was the case for others, only for my situation. I could have very easily been in the other dugout playing against FSU for the right to go to Omaha. Seeing Mark Rose, the starter for the Bulls and my former roommate on the road warming up in the pen reminded me of the very first day of spring 1984 when Coach Cardieri asked the team as a group what our goals were.

Some said individual goals and some said to make the conference tournament. The answers varied, but one stood out. Mark Rose said one word, "Omaha." He understood that all your goals would be realized if you make it to Omaha. Now, our team was in the way for Mark and his teammates to realizing that goal. If they could possibly beat Loynd, then they'd have to face Lewis in the second game, and this wasn't an easy task to complete.

Although Loynd did not have his "A" game, the hitters that night did. Our lineup put much pressure on Rose and their pen to eventually score 11 runs, a number that the pitching staff had given up only two times all year. I had spent most of the second half of that game in the pen warming up to come in for Loynd if he lost control of the game. During the sixth inning, Coach McLeod told me something very inspiring.

"Eddie, you could have been the guy that got them over the hump," Mac said.

Again I thought of all the coaches that preceded Mac and felt the validation of being a part of this team and a true Division I pitcher. Loynd got out of trouble, and as the game got to the eighth inning, Richie Lewis became the closer for us. He finished off Tony Taylor for the Bulls in the ninth with a high fastball, and that was it—we were going to Omaha!

The human pile on the pitcher's mound was epic, and we enjoyed that night like no other! My friend from high school, Brion Cummings, was there to celebrate as well. We partied with all the players and fans well into the evening.

The culmination of realizing a team goal was just as thrilling for me as I celebrated on the field in front of my former teammates. As I spoke with them after the game, they wished me well. They were happy that I was able to succeed moving on to FSU. There was this feeling I had—like my former teammates felt as if I'd quit on them by transferring. Nonetheless, it made me feel good that I was able to get where all teams wanted to go and beat the team I had felt given up on me.

South Florida has never come closer to making the CWS than they did that evening in 1986, and that was over 30 years ago.

We wouldn't be playing our first game for a week, so the anticipation of the play was enormous. There were many arrangements that needed to be made, and we still needed to stay in game shape mentally during the hiatus. The practices were kept light and fun. Pitchers treated their bullpen sessions as if they were in a game. We'd be leaving a few days before the first game to get acclimated with our surroundings, and the players all were excited when the day arrived.

The 1986 College World Series was the fortieth CWS to date, and FSU's first since 1980. Mike Martin took his inaugural team to Omaha after a 50-10 record with high hopes, but came away with a 0-2 record and an early exit. This 1986 team had much higher expectations with a 57-11 record and the top seed at the CWS. What seemed worse was the belief that the Seminoles were by far the best team out there that year and those expectations were hard to handle.

The field was filled with some historically good teams such as Arizona, Maine, and Oklahoma State. We also saw familiar faces Louisiana State and Miami from this season, and Indiana State and Loyola Marymount rounded out the field. Our first game was against Indiana State; it was the eighth seed and was considered a long shot to go far in the tournament.

After an easy victory, we faced our longtime foe Miami. We'd already played The Hurricanes six times that year, and we had split the games at three each. Again, it was pitching that made the difference and Lewis was huge on the mound that day. By winning the second game, we had to face the only other 2-0 team in the CWS, Arizona.

Back before the current structure of the NCAA Baseball tournament, the two undefeated teams would play "Game 11," usually the most intense game of the tournament. The winner of Game 11 would have an automatic bid to play in the championship game against the team from the loser's bracket, even if they lost their next game. With the anticipation of this game and having 20-1 pitcher Mike Loynd on the mound, we felt good about our chances of advancing.

Arizona started future MLB pitcher Gilbert Heredia, and we got to him early. After scoring and then loading the bases, Paul Sorrento hit a grand slam over the right field wall, and we were up 5-0. But that was the last run we scored as Arizona began to pick away at the lead, eventually getting to Loynd and knocking him out of the game in the sixth inning. The score was 7-5 Arizona after some hard hits off Loynd, and the Wildcats managed to tack on two more for the final score of 9-5.

We went back to the hotel in disbelief of how, after having a five-run lead, we could have possibly lost the game. Arizona was a good team, but they barely qualified to play in the regional, let alone win it. Coming out of the loser's bracket is a challenge, but not impossible. The loser of Game 11 would face perhaps the best hitting team in the country, Oklahoma State.

The Oklahoma State Cowboys had always been considered the best college team to play for if you were a hitter. They had Pete Incaviglia last year, and he was replaced by freshman sensation Robin Ventura. Ventura hit .455 and set the Division I record for most consecutive game hitting streak at 57 games. This would be a tough test for any pitcher to face.

What made them even worse was their approach at the plate that was taught by their head coach, Gary Ward. They never let a pitcher get comfortable. Every pitch the hitters would step out of the box, take a few practice swings, and never let the pitcher get into a rhythm. Pitchers would usually get restless, make a mistake, and the next thing you know they plated six that inning.

Chris Pollack would be on the mound for the Seminoles, a tall lefty with a big sweeping curve. The guys on the team nicknamed Chris "Hollywood" for his family's namesake connections in the movies. Chris's dad and uncle were Bernie and Sydney Pollack and had made many movies, including *The*

Natural with Robert Redford.

One particular afternoon, I happened to be at Chris's apartment playing spades with Keith Kidd and Greg Clayborne, and I noticed a bat on his mantle. As I looked closer, the bat said *Wonderboy*.

"Is this what I think it is?" I asked.

"It sure is!" Chris answered proudly.

On the bat was an autograph of Robert Redford and a comment, "To Chris, thanks for all the help during the movie. Uncle Bobby."

Chris had thrown many batting practice sessions to Redford as preparation for the movie, so as to look more like a seasoned hitter. As I pondered this I picked up the bat and started to swing Wonderboy in Chris's living room—just to say that I'd done it. What a cool afternoon that was!

Well, Chris seemed to be throwing batting practice to the Oklahoma State team in the first inning as they proceeded to score two quick runs on a long home run by the shortstop Monty Fariss. Coach McLeod sent me to the pen after the homer, and told me to warm up—fast. After two more players had gotten on and with only one out, Coach Martin decided to call on me to quiet the hot bats of the Cowboys.

I'd later learned that there was a debate on who was going to start, Chris or me, due to the type of hitters OSU had. The Cowboys had beat up left-handed pitchers pretty badly over the year. Chris had been starting all year and pitched extremely well, so he got the start. It just didn't work out that afternoon, and now there I was with bases loaded and one out with two in.

The second pitch I threw was a perfect grounder for two to Bien at short, over to Luis at second—but the throw was in the dirt to Jose Marzan at first, and OSU scored two more. After the next guy grounded out to Luis at second the damage was done, and we were down 4-0. An inning later after a walk, a stolen base, and a base hit up the middle by Ventura, OSU was up 5-0, and things were getting worse.

I stayed in until the fifth inning and we chipped away at the lead to make it 5-4. Richie Lewis came in and absolutely blew away the Cowboys with his 95 mph fastball and a monster curve. We tied it in the fifth after he came in for me, and then went ahead in the eighth for good. The final was 6-5.

We had our mojo back and felt great about the next opponent, Miami. Miami had beaten Arizona in their next game to stay alive. We'd face them in the semifinal game for the right to play Arizona in the championship. We knew it'd be a battle, but also felt that we were a better team. The problem we faced was, who was going to start on the mound? The choice was between me and Doug Little.

Doug had been struggling and had been skipped in his turn to start most of the last half of the season. He was clearly the fourth starter at this point, mostly due to the velocity of his fastball dropping into the mid-eighty range. I had proven to get hitters out, and push the envelope. Plus, my seven-plus innings against Miami—shutting them down—made the decision difficult for the coaching staff. Ultimately, they chose Doug to start with me first out of the pen and Richie to close if necessary.

Doug pitched an incredible game, working us out of jam after jam that included a circus double-play by Luis and Bien off a groundball by Greg Ellena. The play was on Sportscenter highlights for weeks! I threw a game in the pen and Richie entered in the ninth to record another save. We were going to the championship game against Arizona for all the marbles!

There hasn't been a day that goes by that I don't think about that game we played for the championship. The thoughts of what could've been, if it could be different in some way. We went into the game knowing all the trends were in our favor. We hadn't lost a season series to any one team all year. We had not lost two games consecutively to any team all season. Mike Loynd would be on the mound, the Golden Spikes winner for college baseball that year, and he was 20-2. After the game, we would celebrate what I believed was the greatest college baseball team ever fielded, but it wasn't to be.

Arizona started Gary Alexander, who was a right-handed pitcher with very similar stuff to mine. His fastball was in the mid-80s and he mixed in a slider and changeup occasionally. His control that day was impeccable, putting his fastball exactly where he wanted to, and our hitters kept beating the ball on the ground for outs.

Conversely, they were doing the same with Loynd, and after three innings, neither team was doing anything. Then, all of a sudden, fireworks appeared over the horizon of Johnny Rosenblatt Stadium and Arizona started teeing off on Loynd.

It was inexplicable, to say the least. Mike had four different pitches that he was throwing for strikes, but the Arizona hitters were right on his fastball. They scored one in the fourth, then another in the fifth, and again trouble in the sixth. With runners in scoring position, Martin decided to go with Lewis to try to calm down the Wildcats' bats. It only did the opposite. Lewis gave up a long home run to Gar Millay on a curveball that no hitter had ever done before. Like that, it was 6-0 and the understanding that Arizona would win this game was starting to sink in.

As the seventh inning started, Arizona was at it again—now teeing off on Richie. It was like they knew what pitches were coming...unexplainable. Coach McLeod sent me down to the pen to warm up, and two hits later, I was called in to try to tame the Wildcats' bats.

The first hitter I faced was Todd Trafton, a huge player with tremendous power. On a 3-1 count, Todd hit my fastball between Barry Blackwell's legs at third base. It was an absolute rope. Barry handed the ball back to me.

"Ed, I almost died just then. I didn't even see the ball," Barry said.

They ended up scoring three runs that inning to make it 9-0 in the top of the eighth. I came out in the bottom of the eighth and gave up another run while Arizona second baseman Tommy Hinzo set the stolen base record for the CWS against me. I yelled at him as he stood on second with a 9-0 lead that stealing second was a bunch of bullcrap. It was considered disrespectful to steal late in a game with such a large lead. I ended the inning by striking out the most outstanding player of the tournament, Mike Senne, who absolutely destroyed us that week.

Walking off the mound was bittersweet for me. The national championship was out of reach for us. It was also a lesson of how to pray for things. When in prayer you must be detailed in how you ask. I remembered the evening at Flamingo Road just one year earlier saying to myself, "Lord, it would be a dream come true to pitch the last inning of the College World Series."

My prayers had been answered. I was one of two pitchers that season to pitch the last inning of the College World Series. What I learned was that when you pray for something, you need to be very detailed in what you're asking. I should've asked to throw the last pitch!

I believe that sometimes the Almighty Lord listens to prayers and answers them. Sometimes the answer is "yes" and "no" at the same time.

9 CONTINUING THE DREAM

The summer of 1986 was a very exciting time for me. I played on the Tampa Smokers again and pitched flawlessly during the summer season by only allowing one earned run in over 30 innings. We ended up winning our summer tournament and went to Wichita, Kansas, for the NBC Summer League World Series in late July. After we had lost both games in the tournament, it was time to rest for the upcoming fall season in Tallahassee.

There were some interesting things we found out before we arrived in Tallahassee about what happened during the CWS in Omaha the past year. Apparently, the coaches for Arizona had picked up on something that our catcher Ed Fulton was doing. He had apparently been tipping off the pitches we were throwing. This certainly didn't leave a good taste in our mouths, considering it may have cost us the national championship. I did give credit to the Arizona coaching staff for picking it up, though.

We had our first meeting about a week before practices started up and we got to meet some of the new recruits for the 1987 team. With the losses of Loynd, Little, Ashmont, Thomas and Dunn due to graduation and Lee due to injury the coaching staff made pitching the number one priority. From the JUCO ranks, we picked up Jerry Nielsen, Rod Byerly, and Jon Wanish, and also signed Matt Dunbar and Mike Brady as freshman out of high school. Nielsen, Byerly, and Wanish were all starters and elected to compete for the two open starting jobs left by Loynd and Little. Both Dunbar and Brady were expected to mostly learn and get opportunities as they became available.

Well, any thought of cruising into the starting rotation seemed impossible at this point! I was still a walk-on without a scholarship, so that still made me expendable. After pondering this for a couple of weeks, I decided to do something about it.

I felt I was a major contributor to the staff the previous year and wanted to ask Coach Martin for a scholarship of my own. Fact was, my parents were still struggling to make ends meet—doing better, but still behind. It also let me know what the baseball coaches thought of me and if they felt I was worth it. One afternoon before practice I decided to visit Coach Martin and just flat-out asked him for a scholarship. I was dumbfounded when he took all but 10 seconds to agree, and I walked out of his office with a scholarship for tuition and books! Sometimes, all you need to do is ask.

Just getting the scholarship didn't mean I could rest on my laurels. It just meant they thought highly enough of me, and I felt secure that I would be playing next spring. They were even considering going after a redshirt season and replacing the sophomore year that I only had two innings with USF. Yes, things were looking great for my chances to get more starts and playing time for the Noles!

The fall season turned out to be a lot tougher than I imagined. I was slated in the fall to be groomed as a starter, and I didn't fair very well during the JUCO scrimmages. Both Nielsen and Wanish pitched much better than I did and overtook any chances of becoming a starter in the spring. Byerly ended up with the closer's role, which left me in the same position as last year—inning eater and mop up duty. I was disappointed in my performance, but still felt very privileged to be on the squad.

This was also a time where my off-the-field life seemed to be changing, as well. My girlfriend and I hadn't seen each other much over the summer. Although things weren't said, we were growing apart. It was easy to see that eventually we'd break up, but it would be unclear when that would happen. We were friends and had a great time together, but our relationship was running its course for eventually parting ways. During the spring season in 1987, we officially broke it off. We tried to get back together, but things didn't seem right after that. I am extremely happy and privileged to have known her and still stay in touch with her to this day.

I mention this because of the significance to what happened during the spring and the effect it had on my season. After breaking up, I naturally started to see other girls and started a relationship with someone else. I met Samantha shortly before the fall ended and I started to spend most of my time off the baseball field with her.

One of my favorite movies of all time is *Rocky*. There is a scene in it that describes what I was going through. Rocky's trainer Mick tells him of the pitfalls of "relations" while you're in training by telling Rocky, "Women weaken legs!"

This was the absolute truth! The longer we dated, the slower my velocity was on my fastball. When you're only throwing mid-80s, there's no wiggle room for mistakes, and hitters were catching up to it fast. I had the worst outing of my college career against the University of Miami by giving up four runs in less than an inning. Worse than that, I gave up two home runs. I had never in my life given up two dingers in one inning. Ugh...

Naturally, I wasn't very pleased with my performance. After I was done icing my neck, I threw the bag against the wall of the umpire's locker room. Upon the explosion of ice and water all over their civilian clothes, I realized this would not go over very well.

I was called into Coach Martin's office the next morning to find him less than enthusiastic.

"Edward, you understand that this isn't how we're supposed to act as a Florida State Seminole, right?" he said. "Bubba, you're just gonna have to sit this next one out."

I had no defense for my actions and acquiesced. I was grateful that it wasn't any longer of a suspension, and I even thought he might kick me off the team for good. I don't know this for sure, but I think that was the time they decided not to continue going after my redshirt. Looking back, I wish I'd have handled myself better in that situation, but it became a part of who I was. Moreover, it shaped me to think about the consequences before I acted.

I needed to make a change. Although I was thoroughly in love with all the adoration I was getting from Samantha , let alone the things she did for me, I had to call it off for at least the rest of the season. I needed to focus my attention on the team I had dedicated myself to, and she was simply too great of a distraction. Reluctantly, we sat down, and I explained the situation, which didn't sit well at all with her. We went our separate ways that night, and I wonder to this day if we would've stayed together if it wasn't for baseball.

Slowly but surely, I started to pitch better on the mound. I went back to the role of mop-up man and did my job for the rest of the season. This FSU team was certainly not as prolific as the year before. This wasn't a knock on the team at all; last year's team was the greatest FSU baseball team of all-time! This team had younger players and lost the Golden Spikes winner Loynd, and also the runner-up for the award in Alicea.

After the regular schedule was over, we had the Metro Conference Tournament to play, which we were favored to win. FSU had won six of the past seven Metro Conference Tournaments, but this one was being played in Columbia, SC. It was also the first time in seven years that it wasn't being played in Tallahassee. Playing in Tallahassee had been a huge advantage for us, considering all the factors—not traveling, familiarity, and most of all, our fans. Traveling to Columbia in South Carolina's backyard would make this a much tougher task than we had last year.

I had started earning a little more respect from the coaching staff after an outing against UF in Gainesville, coming in for a struggling Matt Dunbar. He had gotten the start as a freshman lefty and that left me a little perturbed. I really didn't have a leg to stand on, so when I got in I was happy to be there. Well, things didn't go as planned as I gave up one good hit amongst a bunch of bleeders to give up seven earned runs. After that, I gave up one hit in the last five innings of the game. We ended up losing 10-5, and I overheard the coaches talk about all the weak hits they got in that crap inning. In any case, it gave them confidence that they could count on me to pitch in the Metro Conference Tournament without fear I would screw up.

Well, it didn't take long for them to send me out. We got a 9-2 lead on Louisville, and I threw the last four innings to get a "technical save" that day. Everything seemed to be working, and

I felt good again. The next day we had a tough game against Virginia Tech. They had the All-American Trey McCoy on their team, and he was on fire practically the entire season. With VT threatening in the eighth inning, Coach McLeod, to my surprise, told me to start warming up. Our starter, Chris Pollack, was going through the order for the third time, and they needed to see a different look. With us down by two, Coach Martin called me in with one out and men on first and third. Oh, and was facing All-American Trey McCoy to boot!

With the second pitch, I induced McCoy to hit a perfect two-hop grounder to the shortstop for a double play to end the inning. It didn't mean much then, to keep the score 4-2. In the bottom of the eighth, we ended up getting three runs from our pinch hitter Steve Taddeo, who hit a home run with two on to take the lead 5-4! After an easy ninth inning, I ended up with the win against Tech, and I was thrilled to be a part of both wins. Little did I know the best was yet to come.

We ended up playing South Carolina in the next contest. They were the top seed in the Metro Conference, boasting a 13-1 record for the season and considered the best team to upset Florida State. Richie Lewis went up against the Gamecocks, and although he did not pitch his best, we ended up winning the game 9-5. Due to a couple of unusual moves by Coach Martin, I ended up playing left field for the last three innings of that game. I guess all the hard work during batting practice running after fly balls all the time finally paid off! I almost had an at bat that game, which would have been awesome.

The win against South Carolina guaranteed us a spot in the conference finals against either Cincinnati or Southern Mississippi, who both had one loss each. We would play Southern Miss first, should we lose they would play Cincinnati in an elimination game, and if we won Cincinnati would have to beat us twice. We were very familiar with Southern Miss, having played them the past two years in Hattesburg, Mississippi. It was historically FSU Baseball's spring break visiting there in the middle of March when school was out. I had pitched against them a few times with mixed results, having one start earlier in the year and not fairing too well against their strong hitting lineup. Nobody was certain who would start the game because technically it didn't matter if we won or lost. FSU was playing for the conference championship regardless. It would create a hardship on the other two teams because their pitching staffs would be depleted before facing us in the final.

It was starting to heat up early in the morning that day. South Carolina in late May can be downright sweltering and this day was no exception. After arriving to the field, we went into our normal routine with stretching and warm-up tosses. The pitchers went through all their pregame rituals as well, which usually ended with some form of running; today would be the same. One of the players I'd had the chance to talk with and had become friends with on USM was Darrin Nixon. Darrin and I had talked before games during the year, as well during the 1986 season.

"So, we get to face you today on the hill," Darrin said matter-of-factly—as if I knew any better.

I looked back at him and replied, "News to me. I better go check with Mac to see if you're right."

I immediately went to Coach Mac, and he confirmed that I was starting the first game. I was completely side-swiped! I had no idea I was starting, and the game was beginning in 40 minutes!

I went back to the dugout and rested for 20 minutes or so before getting ready to warm up as the heat was starting to set in. I knew it was going to be a really hot day, and that I'd need all the energy I had to go at least six innings.

My approach to the game was to get in and out as quickly as possible. The less I stood in the heat, the better chance I had to last. The USM pitcher we were facing was Darrell Lindsey, their ace, and surefire top-ten-round pick this year. It was going to be tough to beat these guys today.

Well, the first two innings went scoreless as I accomplished my goal of making the Eagles hit the ball on the ground countless times to our expert infielders. If they hit the ball on the ground, it was almost an automatic out. Then we pushed across a run in each of the next two innings to make the score 2-0 into the fifth. Their leadoff hitter, Scooter Love led off the fifth with a fairly deep fly ball to the right that centerfielder Deion Sanders got a late jump on, and it landed for a double. After a groundout moving Love to third, he scored on a sacrifice fly to center to make the score 2-1.

After we had made the third out, Deion came up to me. He said he made a bad play on the ball and apologized, to which I said, "Do you know how many runs you have saved me over the course of this year? Don't worry about it!"

He just smiled and helped us score three more runs in the seventh to put us up 5-1, the eventual final score. Although I had some tough situations throughout the game, I managed to get out of them time and again. After the last out the bench cleared and I was getting all the high-fives for completing the game and saving the rest of the bullpen for the final game against Cincinnati. Chris Pollack came up to me as we were wrapping up and resting for the next game saying, "MVP baby, MVP!"

I looked back at him and said, "No way, maybe all-tournament, but not the MVP."

Chris came back, "Two wins and a save...one earned run in? The tournament MVP, baby!"

I just laughed and said, "Well, I hope you're right, but I'm not going to believe it till I see it!"

We had an interesting thing happen right after the game that afternoon as well. It had been about ninety minutes before we'd start the final against Cincinnati, and the Metro Conference Track and Field Championships were commencing in Columbia, as well. As we waited for our lunches to arrive, we all saw Deion leaving the field area toward the track and field stadium. I looked around and saw Steve Winterling, one of the assistant coaches, and asked him what was going on. He said because we were in between games and had time, Deion was going to be the third leg of the 4 x 100-meter relay.

Sure enough, he got there, and FSU won the event with Deion blowing them away on his leg. That day he wrote another chapter of his legend and legacy at Florida State, helping win the double-header for the baseball conference championship by hitting a two RBI-single in the final, and helped the track and field team win the 4 x 100-meter relay to secure the track and field championship. Here was how one journalist described the moment:

May 16, 1987, Columbia, SC—As Will Ferrell said in *Talladega Nights*, "That just happened." That's how everyone felt when Deion Sanders cemented his legend at the Metro Conference Championships in 1987. The Metro would occasionally host the championships for all the spring sports over one weekend and in the same location, and the University of South Carolina was the spot that spring. Deion was playing baseball and running track, and the Seminoles were in the middle of the Metro baseball tournament with a double-header facing them against Southern Miss in the morning and Cincinnati that night. As fate would have it, the dominant FSU track program was having a closer than normal run for the Metro

Championship and a pivotal 4 x 100-meter relay would probably determine the conference champs. FSU track coaches had planned to run the relay without Deion, but knew they needed him and when it was clear that there was a chance Deion could run between games, they sent word to the USC baseball field to find Deion.

Here is where the "that just happened" moment came. Fortunately, the baseball field and track complex were nearly adjacent at South Carolina. Deion literally ran over to the track in his baseball uniform, and jumped into a track uniform. Word spread to the baseball field about what Deion was trying to do, and his baseball teammates climbed the outfield fence to watch the race. Deion flew down the track, managing to both receive and pass the baton perfectly and FSU won the race and secured the Metro title. Deion threw his baseball uniform back on and ran to the baseball complex managing to finish his day with a home run in FSU's 6-3 win over the Bearcats that night. That was a fact.

Many believed that Deion actually hit a home run in the final, but this was an error in reporting—many said they just wanted it to "sound better" as if what Deion accomplished already wasn't good enough.

Chris was right about his prediction, and I did end up winning the Most Outstanding Player award for the tournament that week. Although it was a great personal accomplishment for me, it really took a team effort for it to happen. Up to that point, it was a season for me that failed in accomplishing any personal goals that I set out to do, but the team was able to put me up on their back and give me a day in the sun. Thanks, boys, for all the help that week.

Next was the regional in Tallahassee the following week. We knew this year would be more demanding. We had a six-team regional instead of four, and the 1987 team was not nearly as powerful as the previous one. Our biggest tests would be Miami and South Alabama. Although Miami didn't have the year they were used to having, they were always a formidable opponent. South Alabama had one of the best players in the NCAA that year, Luis Gonzalez, and he was going to be a force to deal with. We had split a couple of games during the season, with each team winning their game at home. That was going to be crucial if we were to beat them in the regional.

Our first test was against East Carolina, and Pollack was on his game that day. He pitched through the seventh inning and only gave up a couple of hits, giving way to me in the eighth.

The demons were back as I gave up three straight hits and a run without getting an out in the inning. Martin quickly came in, and that was that. It would be the last appearance I would make as a Seminole. We won the game, and eventually the regional, and went back to Omaha, but there was much doubt in whether this team was good enough to win the championship. Richie Lewis and Chris Pollack dominated the pitching with Rod Byerly making most of the closing appearances. In fact, of the three games we played in Omaha that year, those three were the only ones who ever warmed up in the pen. When the final out was made against Texas, it was surreal moment. I couldn't believe it was over. Coach Martin lined up all the seniors in left field at Rosenblatt and expressed his appreciation for our participation at FSU as baseball players. Just like that, it was over.

As we made our way back to Tallahassee, I thought about what was next for me. I still had one more year of school to get my degree. Thankfully, Coach Martin decided to let me keep my scholarship until I graduated in May of 1988. There was some discussion of trying to get a redshirt year for 1985, the year at USF that I only pitched two innings, but that talk dissipated after my string of poor outings in the middle of the spring.

I played again for the Tampa Smokers during the summer and pitched well, but it wasn't the same. It'd be a strange fall with no practice to go to each day. After about two weeks, I decided to ask Coach Martin about possibly getting that redshirt from my sophomore year at USF. I was depressed that I couldn't be out there with some of my teammates I played with the previous two years, and hoped Coach would say something positive if I asked.

"Edward, we have already committed your spot to another player. We just don't have the room, and you're already behind in everything. I wish there was something else I could do, but I'm afraid it's just not going to work," Martin said.

Although I knew that's what he'd probably say, I was still devastated that they wouldn't even look into it. Didn't I earn at least the chance to lobby for the redshirt? Why did the coaching staff tell me they would pursue it back in March? The memories of being overlooked by the coaches of Christmas-past were flooding back into my memory.

Before I had the chance to calm down, somebody at the *Tallahassee Democrat* learned that I was disappointed about the situation I was in and wanted me to go on record with it. In my haste, I said to myself, *yes, here is how I can make them put me back on the team. If people knew that the coaches decided not to pursue my possible redshirt, they would look bad.* I thought erroneously. I set up a time to give the journalist a statement of what happened and the details. When it came time to do the deal, I backed out.

I thought about what the legacy would be if I called out "Eleven," Coach Martin's nickname by the players, for not pushing the issue on a possible third year there. How would I be viewed in the years to come? I'd been given this opportunity and made the most of it. Now my time had come to pass—we all have to move on at some point. It was my fault that I didn't push it harder during the time I was there to set it up in the first place. I made no attempt to let them know, and they moved on by recruiting another pitcher to take my place.

I also thought of my past issues in high school involving the media. The story would probably be slanted in such a way in which I wouldn't look good, and things wouldn't change anyway. Over the past 25 years, I've felt relieved that I didn't say anything that day to the *Democrat*, and thankful an article was never written. Sometimes things are better left alone. I'm extremely grateful to all the coaches for letting me be a part of FSU Baseball, and will be proud of that until the day I pass.

In February of 1995, I remembered many occasions where the media was my adversary and my supporter in both high school and college. I've experienced both sides, and the most important thing to understand is what role the media plays in sports. The truth is never understood by those who read and listen to the media—you as the reader or listener have to inject common sense to come to a conclusion on what is really happening. This was never truer than what we would experience the next six weeks in Arizona.

10 FIRST WEEKS OF SPRING TRAINING 1995

The first week of camp started off slow and deliberate with the pitchers not throwing off the mound for the first few days. It was certainly expected that they were going to take it easy on us in the beginning, but I wasn't sure what their motives for it were. The entire organization was divided up into four groups and managed by the head coaches of the minor league affiliates. During the camp, I was put in with the players predominantly in AAA-New Orleans, and Bobby was put into the group with AA-El Paso.

All the groups would get personal attention and instruction from the big league coaches each day out on the field. Garner would visit each group every morning and observe how the players were taking to the drills. He'd talk with the Milwaukee papers about how this spring training was different than the others, openly telling the reporters that some of these players haven't suited up for as many as five years. The last thing he wanted to do as the head coach was to bust these guys too hard and have them pull a hamstring or tear an Achilles tendon. His job was to make sure they would have enough players to field a team for the first exhibition game in a couple of weeks.

Although Garner admittedly told the reporters that some of these guys hadn't played for a while, he also said they were more than capable of playing at a high level. The media was notorious for making mountains out of molehills, and the strike was no different. Any opportunity to disparage these replacements was going to be taken, and now that spring training had started it would only get worse. Garner refused to say anything bad about the players that he saw during the camp, and in fact used complimentary words about their passion, hustle, and determination in wanting to make the ball club that would be heading north. Of course, the reporters didn't want to hear any of that and only wanted to focus on the negative side of the situation.

As players, Bobby and I had no control when it came to what the reporters would say about us. The only impact we could have was a negative one at best. If we performed well, it was because all these guys were poor, inadequate baseball players. For those who performed poorly? That was to be expected. In fact, it was encouraged because it'd only prove their point—really a no-win situation for all of us out there. It makes you wonder why all these guys wanted to be put into this situation in the first place. Most of the players at this point were fed up with the media, and would joke about how most of them were guys who never had the ability in high school to play this game anyway, and they needed some way to stay involved in the sport. I can't say I didn't agree with that.

Playing ball every day was exhilarating for me as I had not

done it for nearly a decade. It was better than being a kid—no school or responsibilities to think about. Working out every day and staying in shape was your job. After practice, I'd get back to the hotel and take a nap, then worry about dinner. After dinner, I'd go out to a sports bar to watch the college basketball games, because the NCAA tournament was going on and you can never complain about that. Simply put, it was a very easy lifestyle!

Bobby and I would like to have spent most of our time in Phoenix doing just that, without any thought to how things were going at home. Fact was that we were both dealing with issues regarding our personal lives. I still had issues with Lisa's parents and the status of the business after I eventually returned from my fantasy camp. Bobby was dealing with a far worse situation as his father's health was rapidly deteriorating.

Bobby's father's bout with cancer was coming to an eventual end as the spring season moved forward. There was the feeling of guilt associated with leaving for Arizona in the first place, knowing that there was a chance he could pass away before it was all over. His father knew and understood this as well, but would not let Bobby turn down the chance to play during the strike. Well, there was always the thought that eventually it happened to everyone, but the realization that the time was close and could happen any day could make anybody anxious.

As for me, I would make my daily calls back home and make sure everything was good. Many of those participating in spring training left their jobs and might not get them back after the players came back. Throughout the process, I had been upfront with Lisa's parents regarding the possibility of getting this chance. Still, I never felt like I had their support in the whole situation. Looking back at where Lisa and I were and the relationship I had with her parents and the business, I believe it was difficult for her parents because I left them with the work. Her father started the business during the time Lisa was attending the University of Florida in the late '80s. It was still a growing business when I became involved in 1990. The more I became involved in the day-to-day operations, the less involved her father would get. Eventually, his input would mostly involve the accounting and bookkeeping, and making sure the employees got paid. When the baseball opportunity came along in December of 1994, her father didn't like the idea of having to go back and do the work. The overall resentment itself verified the feelings of non-support I received during that period.

Eventually, those feelings grew to a point over the time following the strike where I could no longer work for them and started my own business. Running the operation for nearly 10 years certainly helped me in understanding how to run a business. I'll always be grateful for that.

Until we started playing games, we'd mostly work on fundamentals for practice. The philosophy of most clubs was to start off easy and work your way into "playing shape" without pulling any muscles, or God forbid, tear something causing the player to possibly miss the season. Every day, the entire camp would start off by running a few laps around the main practice field at the complex.

Warming up each day as practice began, there is a pregame ritual that is practiced at every level of the game called "Long Toss." Whether you were in Little League or the Major Leagues, you could see 10-15 groups of players all starting about 10 feet apart and slowly throwing the baseball back and forth. The player standing on the right field foul line remains there, and his throwing partner slowly backs up to lengthen the distance between them . After 10 throws or so at the maximum distance, the player who backed up would slowly come back to the other until they felt like they were ready to participate in drills for practice.

There would be no throwing off the mound for a few days, just getting ourselves acclimated to throwing the baseball again. Of course, Bobby and I were ready to go all-out because of our own training regimen, but there were many pitchers there not in mid-season shape to start throwing off the mound 100%. Usually, those were the pitchers in their first couple of years in the organization out of high school. They were just learning how to be professional baseball players and trying to shake themselves from the routines high school baseball.

We then broke down into our groups to work on fielding drills. These were drills designed for the pitchers to work on during the preseason. These would be bunting drills, covering first base on a ground ball to the left side, pick offs to second base, and a few other items to get on the same page with the rest of the team. During this time, all the pitchers who had been doing this since before high school moved like robots on covering first, fielding bunts, and come back ground balls to the pitcher.

After we had completed our drills, we were assigned our prescribed running, which we completed on our own. We would run during batting practice so the pitchers would usually get done before the other players. Even though we were to do the running on our own, it was obvious we'd be observed to see how we did. All the work we did pushing ourselves before coming to Arizona finally paid off as we completed the running without incident. We also knew it'd increase, but certainly didn't want to look bad on the first day. So the day ended with cleaning up, weighing out, and getting our ride back to Dobson Ranch.

During the first week, hitters would only have "non-live" pitching from a coach because the pitchers weren't ready to throw live yet. This wasn't the typical spring because all the players reported at the same time. Pitchers and catchers would usually arrive three to five days ahead of the players. The unusual situation regarding this year was certainly the reason for that.

Around the fourth day into spring training, the pitchers started to throw batting practice to get their arms in shape for intra-squad scrimmages. Every day pitchers would take turns, depending if it was their day to throw going up against the hitters in the batting cages. Eventually, the pitchers would strictly pitch in scrimmages for a more realistic scenario as if it were a game. This was when the fun began!

Here is an inside view of the dynamics of a typical spring training. Because the pitchers and catchers were in camp sooner than the rest of the players, they were ahead of them in terms of being in playing shape. When pitchers start throwing batting practice, it can make them uncomfortable because it's inherent in our genes to not want the other guy to hit the ball hard off of you. So, the battle begins when the pitcher starts cutting the ball or throwing a bit off speed, so the hitter doesn't get solid contact on the ball. Of course, this drives the hitter crazy because he is trying to get his timing down, so it becomes a battle between the two.

After a couple of weeks, this ends as we have full scrimmages between teams and the pitchers no longer threw batting practice. When the exhibition games start the pitchers are usually only throwing in games against the other teams, so only pitchers going through rehab or extended spring training will throw against teammates. In any case, this time of spring training fascinated me because of the interesting position it puts each player in as they prepare for the start of the regular season.

Each afternoon after practice, Bobby and I would get back

to Dobson Ranch, rest, and find something to do for the rest of the day. Although the weather was beautiful during that time of year in Arizona, we didn't want to hang out at the pool like many of the other players. There is just something about sitting in the desert sun that drains the energy out of you. Why take the chance of showing up to camp one morning dog tired because you fell asleep while sunbathing? Most of the time, we'd get into our regular spades game and watch ESPN for updates on the baseball negotiations for the day. Eventually, we would head out to Applebee's and meet up with Susan, our bartender, and watch the NCAA tournament games leading up to March Madness.

Susan Skibba was a student at Arizona State University as an undergraduate law student. We'd have many conversations with her about what was going on during our time as replacement players, like what we were going through, etc. I remember she was very much a fan of the NBA and enjoyed watching and rooting for the Phoenix Suns. She was also very passionate about getting her law degree and eventually making a difference as a prosecutor or a judge. After getting her law degree, she became a district prosecutor for the state of Arizona and was eventually elected as a judge in the Phoenix area.

Susan had a great personality along with her passion for sports. Bobby and I enjoyed our conversations with her. As most law students would, we also had the debates about the strike and why it was such a crossroads for not only baseball, but professional sports, and what the possible outcomes would do for the future. Like many other people who believe that professional athletes were paid way too much for what they contribute to society, Susan also understood their belief in free agency and how the dynamics of professional sports work. It's no wonder that she ended up a judge.

I remember there were times that I thought Susan would make some lucky guy a great wife someday—eventually she married Mark Brnovich, who was elected Attorney General for the State of Arizona. I thought about my own marriage and wanting more support from Lisa and her parents. The conversations we had with Susan gave me the support I needed to make the eventual Brewer team coming out of spring training. The extra encouragement during the times we would talk made a huge difference. Spring training could get to a point where you'd feel like you weren't going anywhere. Then, all of a sudden, we started playing games. All these players that were on the fences needed to finally make their decisions.

Management (Bando, Stanley, and Garner) had made it clear that they needed confirmation by March 1st on where each player in camp stood in terms of replacement ball. On the first day, we were all given a directive on a sheet of paper written by MLB giving us three choices of participation. They were as follows:

1. Sign a replacement contract.

2. Play exhibition games but not replacement games.

3. Participate in spring training but play no games.

Through the spring prior to the first game, many were confused on how to answer the directive. The MLBPA made it clear that any participation in a MLB sanctioned game that collected gate revenue would be considered a "scab game" and you'd be blackballed from ever being in the union. For many of these players who'd been in the minors for years, it was the most stressful time of their lives.

Tim Barker was one of those players. A career minor league player up to that point, he had played at every level in professional baseball. Approaching 30 years old, his window was about as close to closing as anybody else's. He gave an interview to a Milwaukee paper that spring that talked about the stresses that he and many others were experiencing at the time.

"It's not a clear-cut decision for everybody. This is a guy's career we're talking about. I think everyone should take their time and weigh options." Barker said in the interview back in March of 1995. He further added, "I've got a family to think about, so it's not just a decision for me. Every person has a different situation. You have to be honest with yourself. I go one way one day, then the next day it's the other. It's a tough decision. I haven't made up my mind yet."

Brian Givens was another career minor league player who had to make that decision as well. Brian was drafted in the 10th round of the 1984 amateur draft by the New York Mets after his only year at Trinidad State Junior College in Colorado. The big, tall, left-handed pitcher had developed arm issues over his 10-year minor league career that spanned five different organizations before the strike in 1994. Givens was 29 at the time, and like many others, he felt the pressure of the decision.

Ron Rightnower was another pitcher who was at a career crossroads with baseball. At 30, Ron was considered a minor league veteran like Givens, and the decision to cross the line could be made for him. Although quiet and unassuming in person, the coaches and other players described Rightnower's demeanor on the mound as that of a "bulldog." For whatever reason, Ron had been on the cusp for the last two to three years of breaking into the show, but never got the call we all dreamed about getting.

Yet another veteran minor league pitcher in the camp that spring was Scott Taylor; he was looking for one last attempt to make the show. Scott had great stuff, but occasionally had problems locating the strike zone. That spring would most likely be his last before hanging it up and moving on, so crossing the line would be tempting for him.

With a number of other players in the Brewers' minor league organization with similar situations discussing their options about playing (and the number of guys invited to camp specifically to play as replacements), it looked as if we'd now have more than enough players to field a team for the first exhibition game against Colorado. This didn't bode particularly well for me. If they had enough guys cross, my services wouldn't be needed. I didn't worry too much about this for the time being, as the MLBPA and the owners still seemed far apart in their negotiations. I was confident I'd have a role until they reached an agreement. My goal was to obviously break with the team after the exhibition games and go to Milwaukee, but many more pitchers were looking like they'd cross—and that would probably leave me somewhere in the minors at the start of the season.

The second week of camp came to a close and March 1st arrived quickly for all the players. The first game against Colorado was on the third. It looked like we'd have plenty of players. Bobby and I still didn't know what the schedule would be for our pitching assignments, but the bullpen coach Bill Castro told us we should find out at the end of the workout. The last two weeks were easy for Bobby and me, considering we were in shape to begin with and ahead of most of the others because of it. We felt good about our chances of traveling to Tucson for the first game, and that was realized at the end of practice; we would both make the trip. The following day would basically be a day off, and then we'd be ready to go on the third for our first action during the exhibition season.

There were rumors that a minor league players' meeting at the hotel was going to happen before the first game in Tucson because of reports the MLBPA wanted to address their minor leagues about the status of the strike. They were only rumors, but we were anxious to see if this was real or just a ploy by MLB or the media to make up a story to make it seem like the strike was coming to an end. Well, Bobby and I went to sleep that evening not knowing the next day was going to be one of the most pivotal days of the strike to that point.

11 A FEW KIND WORDS

The news was circulating around the hotel that there was to be a meeting held in the banquet room by the MLBPA representative of the Brewers, B.J. Surhoff. The first game would be in two days and apparently it was a last-ditch effort by the players' union to speak with the minor leaguers and get them to not play in the games (whether they be exhibition or replacement) after April 3rd. Bobby and I figured all the MLB reps were addressing all the players at the same time to give them an idea of what these players were thinking as the spring moved forward.

Bobby and I were interested in hearing what this meeting agenda would be about and how aggressive Surhoff would be with these kids in the minors. Our decision was already made and it really didn't matter to us what he or any other major leaguer had to say. It was billed as, "why we are striking?" and, "the issues that are on the table for the future of the MLBPA." or something similar, as I can't remember the exact wording. Looking back, I really would've liked to have kept the flyer that was posted during breakfast that morning in the banquet room, but c'est la vie!

Most all of the players that were staying at Dobson Ranch were in attendance that evening for the meeting that was supposed to start around 6 p.m. Sure enough, shortly after six, Surhoff walked into the room, but not alone. Two other current players, Bob Scanlon and Todd Jones, were also there to support B.J. in their efforts to let these players understand the position of the MLB players' union. All three were dressed in jeans and polos, noticeably none of them were wearing anything that was considered MLB-sponsored gear. They did wear clothing from Nike, I'm sure was part of a signed personal sponsorship package that many players have outside of MLB.

Surhoff started by giving the players a quick synopsis of where the players' union and the owners were at this time. With all of the news surrounding us every day we all had a sense of that. It was clear that Surhoff wanted to look professional and educated in all that was going on to appear logical to the group of young men mostly in their early twenties. Bobby and I, with years of experience in the real world, started to see through the words and knew how Surhoff was just setting the stage and trying to manipulate the kids into not crossing.

"We understand what it's like to be in your shoes, guys. We played in the minor leagues. Many of us played for years before getting to the show." Surhoff said with passion trying to connect with these guys. "Bob, you were in the minors for what? Seven years? We understand how difficult it is for you." Surhoff continued.

"That's why the players are doing this...it's for the future of baseball. We're doing this for you!" Surhoff claimed, as he

appeared to look at every player that he could right in the eyes.
It took great restraint for both Bobby and me at that point to not
bust up laughing! After that little passage, we both slowly turned
to each other and rolled our eyes—what a load of crap. We
thought to ourselves; *there's no way these guys could be buying
this.*

As Surhoff continued, his voice started to become a bit
sterner and more serious.

"Now, the position of the MLBPA considers any baseball
game in which admission is charged is a 'scab game.' You as
players have every right to play in these games, but if you do, we
have the exclusive right to call you a scab."

After this, there was a moment of silence over the room. I
had to give B.J. some credit in how he delivered a line because
his voice seemed to resonate through the room and back up to
the front.

Surhoff started up again to the players in the room, "When
you make the major leagues, you'll never be allowed to join the
players' union. You'll be considered outcasts. Not only you as a
player, but your families as well for taking this position as a scab
player." Surhoff said.

Then, it finally occurred to me what a farce this was. As I
looked at all the players in the room, (about 80 in all) there were
maybe two or three players that had a shot of playing in the
show after the strike was over. None of them were on the 40-
man roster because the strike included them, as well. Surhoff
was trying to scare a bunch of kids into not playing by telling
them, "When you get to the major leagues you'll be an outcast."

I really couldn't believe the audacity of the MLBPA using
these guys as pawns for their cause. Surhoff, Scanlon, and Jones
would be raking in their pensions in 15 years while the guys in
this room would be trying to find their next job saying to

themselves, "How did I get sucked into that crap?"

Here was my chance to finally get some time in front of the coaches for the big team and you wanted me to sacrifice that for you? This was yet another position that was fundamentally wrong with the players' thinking. This may have been the case back in November before the talk of replacements came up. Circumstances changed when the organization asked whether you as a minor leaguer would cross the line and play in those games, because it told the player that the team didn't consider them a prospect. They hadn't done that until then, and not to all the players that were in the minors. If you'd been stuck in Stockton (A-ball) for the past four years, and they ask you to play replacement ball, then the writing was on the wall. If it was up to me, I'd go ahead, take the money and run!

After Surhoff was done with his address to the players in the room, he asked them if anybody had any questions. Charlie Rogers raised his hand and B.J. glanced over and said, "Charlie?"

Rogers had been in the organization for three years and was dealing with arm issues. He wasn't sure if he was going to be able to play, let alone deciding to cross the line if asked. Because of the arm problems, he himself had doubts whether he was considered a prospect anymore by the organization.

Charlie asked, "What about the guys who need to be seen at the next level? We need to be able to show we are still valuable to this organization. What is wrong with playing in the spring and holding out after April third?"

Surhoff said, "You know Charlie, that's a great question and I can't answer that for you. All I can tell you is if you play in games that charge admission—whether they are exhibition or after April third—we will call you a scab. Some players have to take this into account before they make that decision."

The meeting ended and the players dispersed back to their

rooms as Bobby and I headed over to Applebee's to watch the NCAA basketball tournament and talk about the meeting. We both agreed that the union feared the worst if they had the reps come in and try to scare the minor leaguers. It also told us that we'd be there for at least another couple of weeks. We arrived at Applebee's and immediately saw Susan behind the bar. She'd already started to pour us one of our two allotted beers for the evening. We told her that after a meeting like that, we might have a third!

We had a good time hashing it out with her about the unreasonable request the MLB players' union was making to their minor league counterparts, and she clearly sided with us. We told her as we were leaving this was going to be an interesting week indeed, and there'd be more to report after the first game against Colorado.

The next day we all went to camp with the expectation of finding out our assignments for the first game. Sure enough, Bobby and I would both be making the trip to Tucson for the preseason opening game. It was also apparent that the roster for the game was primarily guys who were suspected to be strictly replacement players. It certainly didn't bother Bob or me as we were going to be part of history—the first replacement game of the strike season.

After our workout, we left to go back to Dobson Ranch and just get focused for the next day. Brian Givens was going back to Dobson, as well. Bobby and I were lucky enough to hitch a ride with him back to the hotel. Givey talked to us about playing on the Birmingham Barons during the time Michael Jordan was on the team. The stories Brian had to tell were truly epic, from buying all the latest electronics for the clubhouse to a new bus for the guys. He also talked about MJ and the nightlife of hanging with Mr. Jordan during the summer of baseball in

Alabama.

A few days before the decision, I happened to get a ride back with him and the MLB directive for declaring your intention to cross the line came up in the conversation.

"So... Ed...what are you gonna do? Are you going to cross?" Givey said to me with that questioned look on his face at a red light in the middle of Tempe.

Before answering, I asked him, "What about you? You've been doing this just about as long as anybody."

Brian just had that puzzled look and kept saying, "I'm not sure...in fact, I may just check the paper off at the very last minute. I'm not even sure if number two is an option. You can only check option one or three in my opinion."

After he answered, I told him that the strike was the reason I was in camp in the first place and I had no choice. He had no idea I was strictly signed as a replacement player.

"I thought that you were some guy that they got from another organization that threw ched (cheddar)." he retorted in disbelief. "Where did you play before they signed you?"

I explained to Brian that I had never signed a professional contract, but came very close at one point a few years earlier. He was blindsided by the answer and it was clear that even the most seasoned guys in camp really had no idea who was signed strictly to play as a replacement player.

Eventually, Brian decided to sign on as a replacement player and chose #13 with a very good reason; he was so undecided to check the number one or number three on the directive that he wanted #13 to wear on the team. After the strike was over, Givens returned to AAA-New Orleans until he was the second replacement called up by Milwaukee that year—the first was Ron Rightnower. He also went on to interview with the Seattle Times in July of 1995, explaining that the replacements were a "joke" and the quality of baseball was extremely poor. Years later he recanted those statements explaining the very nature of being in that clubhouse and trying to mitigate collateral damage, and who could blame him?

For players like Barker, the decision was the most difficult. He was 26 at the time of the strike and not on the 40-man roster. With many ahead of him in the organization in the middle infield, he decided ultimately that this was his best opportunity to get to the Brewers Major League club. As the day to declare drew closer, there were others in the same boat who decided to do that as well.

12 FIRST GAME OF SPRING

The morning of March 3rd started out like any other day we were there, breakfast at 7:30 a.m. at the hotel and arriving at the complex by 9 a.m. Bobby and I were obviously excited about making the trip and getting our first chance to pitch in an exhibition game wearing a Major League uniform. It would be a one-and-a-half-hour trip to Tucson. The game was scheduled to start at 2 p.m., so to get there by 11:30, we'd have to leave shortly after getting to the facility. Once there, we put on our uniforms and made our way to the bus that was already waiting in the parking lot.

The trip there was fairly quiet, the players on board were thinking mostly about the impact that this day meant, and how each of us were going to handle the outside influences surrounding the circumstances. MLB through the office of Bud Selig had issued a circular to all the players participating in spring training that year; a list of potential questions that may be asked of us while this strike was going on. It was clear that we would be baited into answering questions about the current players striking: Why are we taking their jobs? How do we feel about being used by the owners and doing their dirty work for them? We mostly wanted to play ball and compete at the highest level without all the nonsense associated with the strike, but also understood that many of us wouldn't have this chance. In other words, it went hand in hand.

When we arrived, most of the guys were surprised to see many fans outside the gates waiting to get into the ballpark to watch batting practice for the Rockies. All the media coverage up to this point was saying how the attendance would be dismal because of the lack of talent that'd be out on the field. We looked at this as a good sign. Maybe the fans really would give us a chance to show them we were really not as bad as reported. Exiting the bus, there was a rope that separated us from the fans as we made our way to the clubhouse to put our spikes on and get something to eat before taking the field for a shortened batting practice session. It was just like any other spring game; people with balls, hats, and bats asking for autographs and such. Some fans were asking us if we were replacements or not—and others actually telling us they would rather have us than the "money-grubbing" players.

I said to Bobby shortly after arriving in the clubhouse, "This isn't what I expected to see."

The clubhouse is considered a sanctuary by the players in all levels of baseball. Whether you're in college or the professional ranks, it's off limits to media, family members, and often the coaches and managers. Basically, it's where the players "hang" and aren't to be bothered with anything. Clubhouses are where the players get the chance to do things that would generally be frowned upon if they were known to the public. Hazing goes on, poker games, drinking all the time, and (yes) players bring women there occasionally, too—just don't get caught! It's the only place of solace where many superstars in baseball get a chance to just chill out and not be bothered.

As we entered the clubhouse at the Rockies' field that morning, everybody found a place to put their belongings. We also found they had supplied us with soup and sandwiches before putting our spikes on to go onto the field. At this point, Bobby and I thought we could certainly get used to this! Before we finished eating and rested for a few before exiting into the dugout, Garner wanted to say a few words to us about this game and what it meant for us to be there.

A summary of what Garner said was this: *After all the hard work we've put into our practices the past two weeks—and seeing how hard you guys have worked—I wanted you players to know that we as coaches for this baseball team are impressed with the way you have handled this awkward situation that MLB is now in. The people in the stands and the media covering this team may want you all to think about this brand of baseball being inferior or substandard to what they are used to. As far as I'm concerned, you're all good baseball players regardless of what anybody thinks and we are committed to making you the best players possible in the time we have to coach you. Let's go out and work hard, have fun, and remember that this is a game to enjoy.*

We hit the field and looked around to find that the place was about half full an hour before game time. Castro got the pitchers together to get our workout in before we were allowed to speak with the fans and sign autographs, which we started getting asked the minute we stepped onto the field. He gave us an idea when each of us would be heading out. I was going to be pitching after Bobby, and he was the fourth pitcher that would be throwing. It was a foregone conclusion that Tim Dell would start. He was the most outspoken replacement player in the Cactus League with more interviews and lines for the reporters than anybody else. Tim got the reputation as a jokester and enjoyed all the attention he was getting during this time in spring training.

One interesting thing happened shortly before game time as Bobby and I were winding down to get settled in. We happened to run into a fan that chatted with us and thanked us for coming out and playing under such circumstances. A rather elderly gentleman in his 60s or 70s we thought, as he said he had been coming to these games for years. He wanted the strike to go on so we could be the guys playing on opening day. I admitted to him that we were most certainly rooting for the same situation, and also told him that these guys playing aren't what the media portrays them. They were good ballplayers, and if the fans just got to know who we were, they might give us a chance!

As the game got started and proceeded into the first few innings, maybe we lost some of the skeptical fans that would give us a chance. It didn't take long for Dell to get roughed up a bit, and before you knew it, the Rockies had a 6-0 lead. The third inning was worse as another pitcher came in for Dell and promptly gave up five more runs and the game was out of hand at 11-0 in the top of the fourth. Everybody on the bench was thinking, could it possibly get worse?

Darrin Reichle (one of the guys that had been signed out of the Valencia camp) threw two scoreless innings before it was Bobby's turn to throw. Even though Bobby had a good camp up to this point, his arm always had a 50/50 chance of hurting, and there was the issue of thinking about his dad, who continued to worsen in Florida. When Bobby came in, it was clear he was having trouble with the strike zone immediately. Getting out of his first inning with three earned runs, he came out the next and loaded the bases. One more run would score before Garner would call on me to try to cool the hot bats of Colorado.

I remember the first player I faced was Sam Ferreti, and on a 3-2 pitch, he hit a ball to right centerfield that dropped for a triple. That was the harbinger of more to come for me. A left-handed hitter sliced one on the leftfield line for a double, a walk, and two weakly hit singles ended my day, and the rout was on. I couldn't think of a worse outcome that could have been written for us.

After what seemed like an eternity, the first replacement exhibition game finally concluded, and the Rockies won the game 24-2. I'm not sure who scored the safety for us, but maybe I can go back and research that sometime. Baseball is funny in some ways, like how a couple of things can go wrong and the outcome looks horrible. The facts of that game were a couple of well-placed hits at the right time made it look worse than it was.

You would think that it'd be a long bus ride back to Phoenix considering the outcome of the game, but it was quite the opposite. I had the sense that a lot of the guys were relieved that this first game was over and we officially got underway with the spring. The mood was upbeat mostly on all the talk about how the media was going to crucify us the next day in the papers and on television. The visions of the fat guy trying to swing the bat in the cage at the tryout in Valencia CC kept coming to mind as the reports of the "epic fail" of replacement ball were on the horizon. Nonetheless, we laughed about how bad the game was, knowing there was another one tomorrow that'd let us forget about this awful one.

The laughter turned a bit more serious as some of the guys started talking about whether they would play if the strike went into the regular season. Only the upper management knew what everybody checked on the MLB directive when it came down to games, but the ones that checked box number two (play in exhibition, but not replacement games) would be allowed to change their minds. Management apparently had enough signatures from guys willing to play now, but nobody was sure if this would be the case on April 3rd when the regular season started in Anaheim.

Kappesser was the catcher for that first game and was quite outspoken on the bus that day. "When that first pitch is thrown on the first day of the regular season in Anaheim, I'm going to moonwalk down in that dugout!" Kappy said with delight. The guys just busted out laughing at that comment. Kappy had a way of saying something that could relate very well with the guys in the room.

After a while one of the other catchers on the bus that day, Bill Dobrolsky, was contemplating his future with the organization. Up to this point, Bill had been in the organization since 1991 after being drafted by the Brewers in the ninth round out of Shippensburg University in Pennsylvania. Although he was in his fifth year in the organization, he had some early success and even had a call up to AAA Denver in 1992. Mostly, he was stuck in the system that found catchers passing by him for the past few years, and he was still most likely going to be starting the season in Class A Stockton.

"This is going to be a great year for me!" Bill said with authority as we were heading down I-10 toward Phoenix. "I'll be starting in El Paso (AA), and soon after that, I'll get called up. Then one lucky break and I'll be playing in the show!"

Kappesser couldn't let that go past without letting him speak his mind. Bob had seen this, in fact lived this, for the past two years himself. He was stuck in the same place as Bill and had seen the writing on the wall just six months earlier when he was starting for the AAA New Orleans team late last season.

"Bill, what are you talking about?" Kappy said sarcastically. "How many catchers have you seen go by you in the past three years?"

Bill started to plead his case to Kappesser. "No, this year is going to be different...I can feel that this is going to be the year..."

Kappy retorted, "How can you possibly believe they are ever going to give you a chance with what you've done so far? You've been stuck in single A now for four years—you should cross and take the money and run. You saw what they did to me, and there comes a time to wake up and smell the coffee!"

Bob never fudged about how he felt. I always appreciated his fresh viewpoint. He always told you the truth and didn't mince words about it. Dobrolsky shrugged it off and sat quietly as the words seemed to sting a little, but still believed that he was going to make the big-league club one day. It's the nature of the minor leagues and the desperation that many players feel to get so close to the show and never quite make it. Kappesser knew when his time was up and only signed back with the team because of the opportunity to play in the replacement games in the big league venues. In fact, soon after the players struck and it was apparent that replacements were going to be needed, his phone started ringing off the hook. He was working as an elevator repairman in El Paso (where he played for AA Diablos, the Brewers' affiliate) when he was getting messages from scouts all over the country to sign as a scab. He decided to return to Milwaukee after reviewing all the offers due to his familiarity with the organization. Now, just weeks before the season was about to start, he was on top of the depth chart should the season start today. Everybody had the same feeling as Kappy, just one day in the bigs would make all of this worth it!

The bus finally rolled into Chandler as the sun was almost finished setting, turning day into night. It was a long day, and most of the guys on this bus were going to have kind of an off day, meaning we would be at camp, but just getting our work in. The game tomorrow would be with a new set of players and pitchers while we would head back to Dobson Ranch to chill out and see what was happening on the strike front. We'd also be listening to the national news on how the first day of baseball with the replacements was and their attempt to find every bit of bad play video to a home near you!

So, the Brewers were, as expected, front and center of all the jokes on ESPN and in *USA Today*. I couldn't say anything to refute their testimonies of how horrible we looked and this was what to expect from these substandard players. A game like that would look bad on any level, so we basically had to ignore all the media and just get back to work on the field. It would be nearly a week before Bob and I would see the mound again. A player, and especially a pitcher want to get back on the field as quickly as possible to erase the memory of a bad outing, but this was not going to happen because we had too many pitchers in camp. Work hard at camp and know there'll be another game, eventually.

Things at home were starting to happen for us as well. For Lisa and me, money was still tight. I sent most everything I was given back home to cover expenses. It could've been worse; we were obviously saving money in some senses because I wasn't living at home eating, driving, etc., and most of my food was supplied by the team. The biggest issue was the friction caused by my absence at the dry cleaning store. Lisa's parents were over this situation altogether, and hoping the strike would end so I could get back to work. Discussions about when I would be back were pointless; it just created uneasiness between the two of us. The only thing we could do was just say that we were doing the best we could and eventually it would come to an end.

Bobby was dealing with much more than I could've ever imagined at this time. After the bad outing, his arm started hurting more, and his father was on the brink of passing away. His stress level must have been off the charts during this time, but his demeanor was as steady as any other guy there. He was quite secretive about his arm troubles, because teams would rather just send you packing than deal with guys that have arm issues. Even though you could get ibuprofen in the training room for free, he'd go down to the drug store and buy his own. Trainers mark down everything a player requests, right down to ibuprofen, so why give them a reason to think you're having problems? Each day, Bobby would try to reduce the activity on his arm and continue to give it a chance to heal. Getting into the hot tub at the hotel and having the jets massage it for an hour would be another remedy during this time. Anything to be ready in four days for your next time on the hill!

Unfortunately, there was no remedy for his father in Florida. Since Bobby had been in Arizona for the previous three weeks, it had been taking a toll on him that he couldn't be there for his father. It was getting to the point that there was the chance that he might not make it through the end of the strike, and Bobby would never see him again. We didn't discuss it very much during the time we were in camp. I think Bob just wanted to focus on the positive things that were happening on the field for us instead of his dad. That was something that Bob had no control over. He also knew that going back to Florida to see him during this time would've made his father upset. Only hoping and praying could be done at this point, and we were all hoping for the best.

The impasse of the strike was continuing to loom over the first week of the season as well. There was a false expectation that the strike would end before the first week of exhibition games were completed, but the two entities were as far apart as ever before. Player representatives were coming out in interviews, stating their disbelief that the fans were coming out to the games and supporting the replacement players to this point. On March 5th, Dave Magadan was interviewed on ESPN and talked about the current state of affairs.

Magadan told an ESPN reporter he felt sorry for the replacement players because they were being used by the owners and cannot believe that the fans are embracing these players because they are just playing for the money.

Well Dave, isn't this what the strike is all about—money? Would you be on strike if you thought you were being paid more than you were worth?

It was becoming more and more difficult to sympathize with why the players were striking in the first place, and the players continued to put a foot in their mouths with every interview they did. More than anything else, they were becoming scared of the replacement players because of the reaction they were getting from the fans. The fans enjoyed the fact that these players didn't play for the money, but for the honor and opportunity to play on the highest of levels. Money was an afterthought, playing one game on the stage was what it was all about.

I read an article about a career minor leaguer named Dan who stated that he had "no chance" of making the show through the current system and would cross the line, regardless of the circumstances. "I've been through the worst of it, the eighteen-hour bus trips, and I'm burned out on the minor leagues. I understand the organization has put more money into the players at my position and I will not be given a chance. If I could just play one day [in the show], it would all be worth it. Then I could let my glove and spikes collect dust and go on with my life in peace."

Could the passion of players like Dan be what the MLBPA was most afraid of? That desire was nothing but a distant memory for all but a few of the current striking players. This was the fear, and the passion will transfer to the fans who can all empathize with anybody who has had a dream.

13 A PLAYER'S BIGGEST FAN

I vividly remember when my dad passed away and not a day goes by that I don't think about him. Back in 2010 at the ripe old age of 45, I had not experienced death in my family as most people do. Because my mother's parents had divorced and remarried when she was six, consequently I grew up in a family with six grandparents. When my father passed, five of them were still living. Realistically, it was the hardest moment I had to deal with up to this point in my life.

My father was by far my biggest fan when it came to baseball. Although he first wanted me to transfer to the University of Florida after my stint with USF, he instantly became a Seminole for life. I know how proud he was when I had spoken with people who knew him and they talked about how he loved watching me play when I was in school. He loved being in that part of my life as a coach when I was growing up in Wilton, whether it was Little League or Babe Ruth as a 16- and 17-year-old player before college. He was also excited about the strike and our opportunity to give professional baseball one more shot and fulfill a dream of playing in the show.

One of the best moments to enjoy while watching any Major League baseball game is when a player gets his first opportunity to play on that stage; his first at bat or pitch as a big leaguer. The cameras always pan back to the kids' family to get the reaction when they perform well on the biggest day of their lives. It's truly a family moment when it comes to professional sports debut as a player. The parents had sacrificed time, money, and emotion as they watched their son or daughter attempt to reach the pinnacles of their sport. I know my father and mother felt that way when I reached the College World Series in 1986.

When my father finally succumbed to the complications of a 26-year battle with cancer, not only was I devastated, I was angry as well. He was only 68 years old and in an age where people are living longer, healthier lives, he was taken from me at such a young age. I felt cheated. No more talks with him on Sunday afternoons or golf on Sunday mornings. What was the most disconcerting was the fact my children no longer had their grandpa. He still lives in our hearts and memories, but we still miss him very much.

On March 7, 1995, Bobby's father succumbed to cancer. Just a few days before he passed away he had to speak with Phil. He let him know that his father was probably not going to make it through the week, and he would have to fly back home. His battle lasted two years, and before we left for Arizona Bobby had spent time with him every single day. I can only imagine the guilt that he felt because of the situation of being 3,000 miles away and there was nothing he could do. Bobby's father wanted him there to compete, and he would've been upset with Bob if he didn't try his best to make that roster. We can't control certain things in this life—and this just happened to be one of those times.

It was starting to make sense why Bobby didn't pitch very well against the Rockies a few days earlier. Pitching is a very mental thing, and focus is critical. I know if we were in Florida, the last thing on Bobby's mind would have been a baseball game. To have to pitch with the weight of the world on your shoulders and focus while doing it was not easy to do. To make matters worse, his arm wasn't feeling very good. With all of this going on in his head, Bobby still went out and performed for himself and his dad on the day he passed.

News came to the clubby just before the game and Bob was scheduled to pitch in relief. With the bad taste in his mouth from the Colorado game, Bobby wanted to perform and let the coaches know he could play with these guys at this level. Phil called his performance as gutsy as anything he had seen by not giving up any runs in two innings. When he was done, the clubby drove him back to the hotel where he packed up a few belongings and made the trip back to Florida.

Bobby was 29 years old at the time of his father's passing. I can't imagine how hard that was—to lose a parent that soon. The times when I feel cheated are the times I think about Bob and his dad. It makes me feel more fortunate. It's how you spend the time you have (and not the amount) in almost all cases, so enjoy the time you have.

With Bobby back in Florida, I would have more spare time for self-introspective activities that included writing and interviewing other minor league players involved with the strike. I had written down some notes starting with the player's meetings and decided to document this historic event as it unfolded in front of our eyes. It was the lead story on the national news every single night, and people wanted to know what was going to happen next. For us players, it was business as usual—and never mind the talk on the media front.

We had a rare day off in the first week. I took the time to get to know a few of the players in camp. Most of the high-draft picks stayed to themselves and wanted to keep themselves away from the group. They understood what was going on, and even the inkling of associating with a possible scab could cause irreparable harm to their futures. What I did find was that most of the guys that were drafted in middle to late rounds or as free agents would work much harder that the high-round draft picks.

This observation didn't surprise me in the least. I'd been saying this for years those that had been given everything in their entire life and didn't have to work for it tended to not appreciate it. For players growing up in rural or suburban settings, this can make it more difficult to adjust to minor league baseball. I've seen kids who were the best players in their leagues, and coddled to the point that they became pompous, entitled brats that expect to be waited on hand and foot. They have talent for sure, but when they get drafted and signed was when the problems started for them. They were thrust into a setting where all of a sudden all the players around them were just as good—some even better than them—and it was hard for them to get a grip on how to succeed. Our job as parents and coaches is to teach our kids and students life lessons needed to be successful. People aren't going to just give you a job or pay for everything; you have to earn it! I never understood why coaches and parents coddle the best players on the team and don't make them work for it. Those are the kids that should work the hardest! Instead, coaches and parents are lenient on them and down the road, it bites them in the ass.

It makes me wonder about the future of this game I love—

the game of baseball. I'm talking about where it's going to be in 20 years and how it can sustain itself. After Bob had left for Florida, I found out my next pitching assignment would be against Oakland on the ninth. I was excited to be on the list to pitch as my turn was skipped due to weather two days earlier, and I wanted to get the bad taste out of my mouth from the last outing.

The team arrived at the A's facility and got into the clubhouse for lunch before heading out to the field. After getting in our mandatory running, I happened to have a conversation with a lady from Chicago who was visiting Arizona on vacation. She asked me if we were going to have baseball this year because of the strike.

I replied, "Yes, we will definitely have baseball this year. Whether it is with the striking players or with the replacement players, were are going to have baseball this season."

After speaking with her a few moments, it was easy to realize that she was more sympathetic to the owners than the players and just wanted to watch baseball. She went on shortly after that to say she was a neighbor of Glenn Robinson, the basketball player who just signed a $100 million contract.

To that I said, "Nobody in professional sports is worth a hundred million bucks—especially some player who hasn't laced up his shoes in the NBA yet! Larry Bird doesn't even make that much!"

Of course one of the items on the board for the strike was the salary cap and how the MLBPA wanted nothing to do with any cap. The more money, the better, when it came to the minds of the players.

My second outing, which was against the A's, went much better than the first (as if it could possibly be worse). I pitched one inning and gave up an unearned run against the 1-4 hitters in the Oakland lineup. What marked it being a good outing was that I had much better control and I put the ball where I wanted. It was a great feeling to know that I had success in this venue, and I could succeed against an opponent. After that game in Tucson, I started to wonder if I really did belong. It was a long six days between outings, for sure. There was way too much time to think about the disaster against the Rockies. It only went to show that you can't get too high or too low in this game. It was the steady person who stayed in control!

That evening as I thought about when my next opportunity would be, I figured I'd have two more times on the mound before they made any cuts. Rumors were circulating that the Brewers still didn't have enough commitments to field a team on April 3rd, and that suited me fine. We were into our third week, and we hadn't played any intra-squad games to that point because the players' union forbade any to be played with the strike commencing. Well, the coaches decided to start having them anyway because the minor league clubs needed to get ready for the season regardless of what happens on the big stage. The pitchers needed to throw in game situations, and there were just not enough games to get all the work in—let alone those guys in the lower minors that don't want to get in the middle of all the strike talk. The coaches were also worried about pitchers getting arm injuries, so they pulled the trigger with the intra-squad games.

We started to have complications due to the weather over the next week, and opportunities were starting to get slim. I was scheduled to throw in another game on the 12th, but my turn was skipped, and I'd have to wait again. Situations like this would usually bother me, but I realized the strange circumstances we were in—and how it didn't pertain to me. I also understood that under normal circumstances I'd probably be pressing shirts in Clearwater, so that made me feel better, too.

I had a conversation with another player in camp that week, and he asked me an interesting question, "What was the one thing about spring training that has surprised you the most?"

He kind of caught me off guard, but I was glad that he asked. I replied, "It's the amount of running that we're doing. I thought we'd do much more than this. It seems as if we're running to maintain shape rather than get into shape."

Some of the AAA pitchers started talking about the horror stories of years past when it came to running during spring training month. Givens was talking about one year with the Mets, "You were on the field for your two-mile run at 8 a.m. or so, then practice until four p.m. with one break for lunch. After practice was over, you would run another 40 to 50 poles before you hit the showers."

Good God! There was nothing like that going on here.

Givey continued, "One time, the pitching coach got upset with a few of the pitchers and told them to run 100 poles after practice. They had the trainers in golf carts handing them water and making sure they ran every one of them!"

For those of you who are unfamiliar with what a "pole" is, it is running from the left field foul line to the right field foul line in a semi-circular fashion along the warning track of the baseball field. When a player ran from one foul pole to the other, that would measure one "pole." We weren't running anywhere near that amount. Not to say we weren't running at all, but I can't say it was hard.

After thinking some more about the player's question, I said to him, "I'm also surprised about how many pitchers in this camp have about the same stuff as I do. I'm even more surprised by how many of them don't even know how to throw a change-up!"

I couldn't think of where I'd be if I didn't throw a change-up. That's a pitch that you'd throw about 10 mph slower than your fastball. You hold the pitch with your last three fingers with the emphasis of pressure on the ring finger. When thrown correctly, it comes out of your hand with the same arm speed as your fastball, but the physics of the grip and how you hold the ball will lessen the speed. It'll also have spin that will cause a downward movement, making the ball even harder to hit. I believe it's the most important pitch to have in your repertoire.

The only thing I could figure on why these pitchers didn't throw change-ups was that they didn't want to work hard and develop it. They like their 93 mph fastball and 12-6 curve, and no pitching coach is going to tell them any better. *Laziness will eventually get the best of them*, I thought. One day after getting roughed up by another team (and teeing off on your fastball because you couldn't control the curve) only led you to eventually getting released. Having more pitches gave you security, your stubbornness would get you released! It went back to when they were in high school, and they could just blow the ball by everyone. The change-up was a sign of weakness—it meant you didn't believe in your ability to strike batters out. It felt good knowing that guys that had been professional pitchers for upwards of seven or eight years didn't know how to pitch any better than I did.

It was the week of March 12. I spoke with yet another player facing a crossroads in his career. He signed and checked the third option (which was to not play any games during the strike), but was now being pressured by management to signing a replacement contract. I told him in confidence that I wouldn't reveal his name and he agreed to speak with me on those terms. I wanted to hear what he had to say at that point because this pitcher would have a direct impact on me should he decide to cross.

He said the Brewers had been very good to him, supported his family, and he owed them a lot. I could tell by his voice that it was really troubling him on how to go about this decision. I thought that this guy had the ability to make the big club, a true prospect in the organization that shouldn't need to cross, but the combination of his doubts along with the guaranteed money he would get made his decision awfully tough.

It was clear that the Brewers were starting to be aggressive in getting some name players to cross and offering some big money to do it. It was no secret that should the season start with replacements they would be guaranteed $30,000 by the organization, and it would only start there. It was to be the proration of the MLB minimum salary and there would be another $30,000 waiting as the season went forward. This was the case for the guys that were strictly replacement—not the guys they could entice that were prospects. They were being offered more; we just didn't know who or how much money it was.

Speaking with him made it clear to me what the toughest part for him was all about—the game of baseball itself.

"I hate it. I know I'm a good player and if things work out, I will be able to take care of my family and our future. But if I take the money now, and I'm good enough, it'd affect my children, and I wouldn't be able to provide for them. If I didn't have them, it would be easy. But it's not enough [money] for me and my family to retire on. Ed, the game can really sour on you, all the stuff that goes on. Once I'm done playing ball, that'll be it for me. I just hope I can make enough [before] my arm falls off," he said.

Money had changed the state of the game. This was the depressing thought that permeated my mind as he spoke to me.

Back in the '60s and '70s, the game seemed so much different. The Big Red Machine and the '69 Mets were two of the reasons why baseball was so popular, and now the personalities of the players have changed, and it seems for the worse. Fans are the people who paid your exorbitant salaries, the ones that you wanted to play in front of and entertain. They owe you. You (the players) don't owe them anything anymore. Don't even ask for an autograph; it'll probably cost you. This strike is all about making sure we'd get paid regardless of how it ultimately affects the very fabric of the game.

14 SEDONA (THE EPIPHANY)

With almost three weeks left before opening day, there was still a lot of doubt that there'd be significant progress in the negotiations for a settlement. Bobby and I set out for our usual meal at Applebee's on March 14th. We wanted to see what ESPN was reporting for the day's events. After a rundown of the action they showed (which of course had all the poor play and none of the good), Keith Olbermann produced a parody of the classic skit "Who's on First?" by Abbott and Costello.

Bobby and I watched in disbelief as Olbermann narrated the parody of propaganda with some of the most blatant misreporting of journalism I had witnessed to that day. There again on center-stage was the guy from the Valencia tryout who lasted 30 minutes before being told to leave. Play after play of errors, missed baseballs by hitters—with the background of Abbott and Costello saying those famous lines we all know so well. After Olbermann's self-absorbing moment had come to an end with the skit, he talked about the shortstop on the fictitious

St. Louis Brown's team whose name was "I don't give a darn." In obvious amusement Olbermann said, "This is the player that I'm most interested in," with sarcastic overtones.

It was embarrassing to think that ESPN was trying to gain popularity by showing their disapproval of the current situation between the players and owners. Especially in such a manner that disrespected players that have played professionally for many years. This was why newspapers had editors who read their journalists' articles before they were left for human consumption. ESPN was more interested in being another *Comedy Central* or *Saturday Night Live* when it came to news about sports.

Back in the late 1970s, ESPN started out as a "fringe" network that'd broadcasted many of the sporting events that NBC, ABC and CBS wouldn't. They were sports like Australian Rules football, NCAA College Baseball World Series, and other non-mainstream sports. Slowly, the anchors were gaining popularity and becoming household names by their peculiar mannerisms. They were eventually given the latitude to be humorous when reporting the day's events. Easily the most famous of those anchors was Chris Berman. His All-Star Home Run Derby calls of "back, back, back, back, back—gone!" ended up being legendary. His description of professional athletes' names by using his own nickname for them was equally as famous.

Somewhere down the line between 1980 and 1995, there was a disconnection between reporting and opinion with ESPN. They became more interested in making the news instead of reporting it. Newspapers had editorials that gave an opinion about subjects that might be particularly moving at that time. Readers understood that it was only opinion and were given a venue to respond. With ESPN, there was no venue to respond and most items reported were slanted to their viewpoint without equal time. I compare it to that radio host on a local station that takes callers. If he didn't like your opinion, he'd just hang up and then blast you for calling.

I thought about how Olbermann and others had totally and thoroughly disrespected those players that played in the 1995 spring before the strike ended, and how it left a scar on his reputation, in my opinion. If I only had a moment to say something to him or ESPN in regards to the coverage that spring, it'd be this: If you didn't want to support the guys that were playing those games, fine—just report the game and be on your way. Don't use these guys for your own agenda and make us appear to be a bunch of oafs that didn't belong on a baseball field. It wasn't a label they deserved, especially when many of them have dedicated over 10 years of their life to the game. They deserved your respect, regardless of the relationship the reporters had with the MLBPA.

Well, Bobby and I certainly didn't care much for the parody. Susan laughed and told us anybody in our situation was just going to have to deal with media, whose only concern is their own agenda. We had no control on what they reported and could only do our best when it came time to play in the games. The fans that came out to see baseball that spring knew we could play at a high level and competitively. The Brewers had been doing well after the disaster in the first game. The guys had some fairly popular players getting articles written about them. If the strike wasn't going on, it would've been considered a really good spring to that point for the Brew Crew.

The games moved forward, and I made my second consecutive improved outing against the Angels. Tim Dell started the game. I came in for him in the fourth inning with men on second and third, with one out. I ended up getting us out of the inning without a run crossing the plate, giving me the boost of energy that I greatly needed. I pitched one more inning after that, and ended up giving up a run because I made a poor pitch selection. All in all, an acceptable outing—and I felt as if my stock moved up with the coaching staff. Every time you pitch wasn't going to always be perfect. The guys hitting against you were working their asses off, too.

The bus ride back to Chandler was once again filled with banter about the season starting with us in Anaheim on April 3rd. We'd been playing for three weeks, and there had been virtually no movement from both sides. There were still rumors around camp that we didn't have enough players to start the season and management may start enticing guys to cross the line. I was hoping that wouldn't happen, obviously because my future would be dependent upon it.

Fred Stanley gave the players that played in the Angels game the next two days off, and that was well received by all of us on the bus. We hadn't had a day off in two weeks and could use the break in the action. Most of the guys that had the day off went out that night, regardless of the midnight curfew set by the organization. Most thought nothing of it, considering the next day was an off day. As luck had it, they did check curfew that night and a bunch of the minor leaguers got fined $50 for the offense. A second would cost them $100, and a third would be to get sent home (although all the vets said they had never checked more than twice during the spring). The replacement guys (including myself) who got caught didn't have to pay the fine, as we were already considered with the big club now. I was happy about that, and I really didn't have the $50 to give them at the moment, anyway. I'm glad I didn't have to deal with the repercussions of having to tell Lisa why I got fined either.

Most of the guys used the day off to catch up on sleep or

play some golf. I couldn't get a tee time, and preferred to sleep at night, so I rented a car and went to visit Sedona, Arizona for the day. It was only a couple of hours north near Flagstaff, and it provided some spectacular views of the native landscape. I would've liked to visit the Grand Canyon, but it was simply too long of a drive for a short period of time off.

Trips like the one I made that day are extremely important for me. It gave me time to think about what was going on in life...meditation behind the wheel, I guess. There were many things to think about, like the next opportunity to pitch. This would be the most critical by far. What was going to happen after the strike ends? Could I get another contract? Sometimes I'd find myself saying, *what the hell am I doing out here 3,000 miles away from home? All for this pipe-dream?*

There was much to think about during my drive up to Sedona that day. With more of the Double A and Triple A guys starting to figure out that this may be their only shot of playing in the show, not only was I less likely to make the team, but it also created more leverage for the owners to have the players' union cave to their demands. Either way, it made me expendable (and the other guys signed strictly as a replacement). After a while of these thoughts running through my head, I arrived to my destination.

I would've liked it to have been a little bit clearer that day—also ironic due to the cloudiness of my thoughts on the ride there. I was able to buy one of those "panoramic" cameras that could get a much wider view, but to no avail, as they came out hazy. Weeks later when I got the pictures back, I was happy that I bought a few postcards with perfect pictures. "What a rip off that camera was," I thought! You think you're doing something to make things better and you're only making them worse. Sounds like the owners and players.

I knew some way, somehow that this strike wouldn't last very long into the season. We as the replacements only cared about at least starting the season. For us, it was about dressing for one game. For us, we'd realize a significant part of our persona. It was more than checking off a bucket list, it was validation that we competed at the highest of levels on the biggest stage. Just being part of this spring playing with Milwaukee had given me the validation that I could compete with seasoned professional players. Even though they (and other teams' players) weren't on the 40-man rosters, that by no means made them bad players. They were the very best players in the world. I competed and had success, as well as failures. That was the nature of the game.

I felt as if there was a weight lifted from my shoulders after pondering these thoughts. The drive back to Phoenix was tiring as the mental fatigue set in over the day. I got back to the hotel and spoke with Bobby about the trip. He had gotten back from Florida a couple of days earlier and all the stress related to his father's passing was beginning to subside. He didn't talk much about his trip back and the events. I wasn't about to pry into his head about everything. I'm sure he just wanted to concentrate on getting back into the routine.

I told him I started writing down notes each day and spoke with players about their feelings with everything going on. He thought I was joking about writing a book about this time in baseball. I wanted this time to be remembered for what it was and how it affected the people in the game, as well as us. I wanted there to be documentation of possibly the most trying time in baseball history. Someday there'd be a time when nobody remembered what these guys did for the game, and it shouldn't be like that. Our small part in the advancement of this game should be respected. I wasn't ashamed of the part I played in this, and neither should any of these guys for choosing to play. They all should be commended—not condemned.

Bobby was a little surprised that some of them opened up and talked about their situations, even when in confidence. Most players were pretty private and kept to themselves. For some of them it had a rehabilitative effect, an outlet to speak their minds with no judgment. Players in the minor leagues are often thought to live this glamorous lifestyle, with their fancy automobiles and jewelry, going on extravagant trips and spending lots of money. Very few of them sign for huge sums of money after they get drafted, and most are just struggling to stay in the game. Most of the guys they signed after high school got sent to Helena or Beloit (Low A) and lived the life of 15-hour bus rides combing the countryside. Their salary is about $750 per month, and they got around $8 per day in meal money when on the road. For the players that were top-round draft picks and didn't blow all their money already, they could use a little of that to live on—but the rest of these guys were just struggling to get to the next level. Sounded glamorous to me...

Another player I spoke with gave me his testimony about how this strike changed the way he viewed his family and baseball. "I played with the Mets for six years before I signed with the Brewers, and I devoted my life to the game. Last year after spring training I gave it all up," he said. "I hardly knew my wife and kids because the whole time they were growing up I was out of town playing baseball. This past year I became reacquainted with them, and it made me feel better about myself, and that's what is important."

The more I spoke with these guys, it seemed like this profession was more of an obsession, an addiction. They loved the game, growing up with the belief that it holds happiness in the cards for the rest of their lives. The vast, vast majority of them never participated in a spring training, let alone played in the show. The longer it goes on, the further their dreams became—until the desperation set in for life.

"If I had only done this, or done that...If I played in that organization, I could get a chance. Why won't they respect my request for a trade and give me a chance?"

The thoughts of these guys made me think about how lucky I was to be in this position playing this spring. Many of these guys spent over 10 years reaching this same very spot I was sitting in—10 years! We were blessed for sure to be here, Bobby and me. I'll always respect every one of those guys who put on that uniform in the spring of 1995.

St. Patrick's Day wasn't as exciting as it would've been if I were at home in Florida. Being 25% Irish, my family would treat this day with the greatest of respect—meaning we'd be having a great time drinking Irish coffees and tilting back a few glasses of Guinness. We were paid meal money for the next three days, which meant we'd be here for at least that amount of time. The word on the grapevine was they still didn't have the amount of players needed, but management was upping the ante for them to cross. Bobby and I believed that we'd be here now until at least the thirtieth, depending on how the minor league players reacted to management's efforts to get them signed-on. Again, we had to take the excruciating wait and see attitude for the time being.

I found out my next opportunity to pitch would be the following day (the 18th) against California. What I did on the field was most important. Sometimes the best players fail and don't make the squad—and I had to realize that. I was the only player in camp with zero pro experience (which still made me expendable), so there was no time to have a poor performance. It was like being a walk-on in college all over again; you must work harder and play better than the others out there. Then you hope and pray that the coaches saw enough character and guts along with your ability to give you a shot of playing in a big game. Still, after all of this, I had to remember that the odds were against me making the team. No matter the final outcome, I'd already proven I could play at this level—there was nothing left to prove.

15 EVERYONE HAS A NICKNAME

Looking back at the entire time we were in Phoenix, I'd realized that weekend was the best time I'd have in a Brewers uniform. We had our game against California on Saturday. I was called on in the seventh inning to pitch and performed well—almost too well. I was able to retire the side in order and only threw 12 pitches in doing so. It was a day a pitcher dreams about—my fastball was as hard as I had thrown all spring. The coaches said I was reaching 87 to 88 mph on the gun, which was great for me. My slider and change-up were working great as well, giving me three pitches to use to get hitters out.

Upon approaching the dugout after the inning, Garner came to me and said, "Great job, Ed! Right [Rightnower] needs to get the last inning so you can ice down if you need to."

I looked back in displeasure at Phil and pleaded my case for another inning.

"Gar, I only threw twelve pitches! I can go another inning,

and I need the work. I'm just getting warmed up!"

Garner saw the displeasure on my face and in my words and acquiesced somewhat. "Ed, is your arm strong enough to go tomorrow in Tucson if we need you?" he said with eyebrows heightened.

"Absolutely! My arm never hurts...I don't ice, take Advil or use Sportscreme. I've been pitching for nineteen years, and I've never had a sore arm. Of course I can go tomorrow!" I proclaimed back with conviction.

With that retort the entire coaching staff was on the floor laughing. I think they thought that I was telling them that my arm was never sore even after throwing nine innings at one time, and that wasn't the case. What I was trying to say was that I'd never had issues with my arm and it was resilient. I was trying to convey to them that I had a rubber arm and could pitch two, three days in a row without any issues. This would make me more valuable because not all pitchers could do that.

With all the laughter by the coaching staff and earning respect from the players, I started to feel like a part of the team. Before that weekend it had seemed I hadn't quite made it over the hump, so to speak. Bob Kappesser started nicknaming me the "Porsche Man" due to its similar sounding linguistics. Then he shortened it to "911," after the Porsche model.

"In an emergency, the Brewers are going to call the Porsche Man-911!" Kappy would laugh as he was saying it.

"If I were your agent, Ed, I'd work a deal with Porsche and get them to give you the model of your choice—for a small administration fee, of course!"

"Sounds like a good deal to me, Kap!" I said proudly.

In baseball, amateur and professionally, nobody calls you by your real name in the arena. Because of Bob's shaved head, playing catcher with the last name Kappesser "Kappy" was born.

Bobby Cuff has been called "Cuffer" or "Rotator" pretty much his entire baseball career.

Then there were the nicknames that really made no sense at all unless you knew the story behind them. One game early in the spring season, Bill Castro caught me with my watch off, timing the opposing pitchers from delivery to home. This was done to help make decisions on whether you'd have the player on first try to steal second. The longer it took the pitcher to get the ball delivered to the catcher, the harder it'd be to throw the runner out.

"What are you doing?" Bill said to me with a puzzled look.

"I'm just seeing how long it takes for the pitcher to get the ball to the catcher. I haven't gotten a time yet from the catcher throwing to second, but if we try to steal, I'll see how quick he is," I said without looking at Castro.

"Watchman!" Bill said with delight.

Castro just shook his head and laughed after anointing me as the "Watchman." Sometimes it was as easy as that, but nobody outside would understand it without the explanation.

Later that day, Garner told me that I'd be with him during tomorrow's game. I was completely psyched to know that I was the only pitcher in camp to throw in games on two consecutive days. That was meaningful. I was going to make sure that I got there early, took care of myself, and did not screw this opportunity up. I went to bed that evening thinking about the next day and another chance to pitch in a big game.

I was able to get a lift from Givey to the facility. We had to get there early because the bus left at 8:45 a.m. to go to Tucson. When we arrived, I knew we had "split-squad" rosters because of two games being played by Milwaukee, one in Chandler and one in Tucson. Garner said I was going to be with him in Tucson so I double checked the rosters to see if anything had changed, it hadn't, and my name was on the list for Tucson. After checking, I went to my locker and started dressing when Bob Kappesser came up and started buzzing the locker room about me making the trip.

"Look at the Porsche Man making the trip to Tucson!" bellowed Kappy with surprise and humor.

"It's a good sign for you if they're giving you this opportunity to throw consecutive days—you know that right?"

I told Kappy humbly, "I'm just happy to be here and glad they are giving me the chance to throw again."

We got on the bus and started down the road when I noticed that Garner was missing. I thought to myself that he takes his own vehicle sometimes and he'd be there when we arrived. Soon after we got there, I ran into Castro, who was looking at me as if I had a third eye in my forehead.

"What are you doing here?" Bill said in amazement.

"Phil told me yesterday to be with him in Tucson...I thought he'd be here. I checked the rosters before we left and nothing had changed," I replied.

"Phil is coaching the team in Chandler today...we have seven pitchers here in Tucson and only five there now. I'll try to get you in today, but it'll be tough. You may only be throwing a bullpen if I can't," said Castro.

Great, just great...I just blew my one chance, I thought. I finally had the chance to prove to the top coach in the organization I was valuable enough to make the squad on opening day. Why weren't the changes made on the board? It clearly said that Garner would be coaching in Tucson...or did it? Maybe he was to stay in Chandler while the other coaches went to Tucson. Whatever the case and whatever the sheets said, I now look like a 19-year-old idiot who can't read.

Well, I was just going to have to hope that some way I

might get into the game. Throwing a bullpen session was fine, but you can't replace real innings against hitters. There was no way to duplicate it. *Time to forget the past and settle in for the game.*

The game began with the starter throwing four innings and then another pitcher struggled with the next two-thirds of an inning. My roommate Brian Tollberg got the last out in the sixth and gave way to Stacy Burdick in the seventh. I was in the bullpen trying to decide when to get up and throw because there were three pitchers left and only one or two innings available. It didn't take long for Stacy to get in trouble with his control. Myself and one of the other guys started warming up in the pen and I thought for sure I was not going to get into the game.

When Stacy finally finished the inning and was walking back to the dugout, I saw Castro pop out and look into the bullpen where the other pitcher and I were warming up. When Bill pointed to his wrist indicating a "Watch" I knew instantly he was calling for me to pitch the last inning.

Immediately my heart started pumping as the rush of adrenaline went through my veins! I honestly thought I wouldn't get into the game, but Castro decided to give me the last inning anyway. This day seemed different—like the one I had in the first outing at Florida State. I thought, whatever you do, don't mess this inning up because Bill went out on a limb for you.

I came in and was throwing as hard as I was the day before. All my pitches were working, and I felt good. After giving up a swinging bunt and a walk, I was able to get out of the inning successfully. Another outing without giving up an earned run and I really needed it. We were getting closer to the end, and the coaches were making their decisions over the next week on who would be going "North" to Milwaukee. If they still didn't have commitments from the guys in AA and AAA to cross, I most certainly would be in the mix.

After the outing against Colorado, I decided to move my things over to the Major League clubhouse at Compadre Stadium. I felt like it was important that I stay with the coaches on the big league team and just act like this was a done deal. I think in the business world they call it the "Assumption Close." I'm just going to make the assumption that I'm on the team until I was told otherwise.

The practices at the minor league complex had gotten simple. Basically it was get your arms loose, batting practice, run, and then hit the showers. Even if you needed to lift, you were done by 1 p.m. I didn't want to be lumped in with the minor league players any longer, because in the end they would be moving on to their assignments within a week. The minor league players would be off to Helena, Beloit, Stockton, El Paso, and New Orleans, while the replacement team headed for Anaheim. My time with the minor league coaches was done and it was time to stay with the replacement team until told otherwise.

I had the chance to speak with Ed Durkin that day. He'd been keeping a close eye on us via the newspapers and the word out on the street from his peers about our progress in Arizona. He had said that he'd be here last week, but the Brewers sent him to Texas for another assignment. We talked quite a bit about the players in the camp with me, and he gave me some background on where they were from and what they were all about. I gave him the inside perspective of how camp was going and what the players and coaches were going through. Ed was surprised and found it hard to believe that the coaches didn't know certain players were here strictly as replacements.

That was the week Bobby Cuff was working with the AA El

Paso pitching coach as they approached the end of the spring. Rob Dirksen was talking with Bob about how if the strike was ending he would be with their club in El Paso for the start of the season, and he would be one of their starters. Dirksen wanted him to continue improving his change-up because the hitters in that league had always been ahead of the pitchers. Bobby filled me in on parts of his conversation with Dirksen.

"Dirk," Bobby said, "Look at me...don't you know why I'm here? I signed as a replacement player out of Tampa."

Dirksen replied, "You're kidding me, I had no idea."

Bobby told Dirksen about his position with the VA hospital at Bay Pines and how if the strike ended he'd most likely go back to it. At 29, Bobby knew the future plans for the Brewers would most certainly not have him in it. For many seasoned minor league veterans, the road would be hard enough to make it after the strike was over. They had at least paid their dues with the long bus trips and years in the minors. Somebody like Bobby? Not only would they ignore him, but it would be downright vicious because they wouldn't respect a guy that didn't pay his dues. It would be similar to millionaires giving respect for the person who won $60 million in the lottery. What did they have to do to make their fortune? Buy a ticket and get lucky? The MLBPA would make his life miserable.

Durkin indicated to me that he was really pleased with all the guys he was able to sign out of the Valencia tryout. He made the point that he was pleased with how I had performed up to this point and I should make the team if we started the year with replacements. There'd be other factors Durkin reminded me of, including the chance that more minor league players could start to cross, which was most concerning. He also said I needed to continue being a stand-up guy and continue to hustle my ass off. I was determined not to embarrass him for taking a chance on me. We ended our conversation with indication that Fred Stanley was having a meeting for the replacement players the next day and we'd be finding out what will transpire over the next couple of weeks.

After speaking with Ed, I was feeling pretty good about the entire situation that was coming to an apex the following week. I'd performed well enough to be in the mix, and we were finding out all the details for the start of the season tomorrow. I figured I'd have three or four more outings before camp broke. Some may be in minor league games because they canceled the last two MLB spring training games due to the players' union. I still couldn't afford to have a poor outing, and I was going to do what I could to keep myself ready each day. The next day would prove to me the truth in the saying, "You can't get too high or too low in this game." I would find myself searching for the truth about where I stood with the organization.

16 REALITY SETTING IN

Have you ever had the feeling that you were in a room full of people and you didn't belong there? It is a disconcerting feeling. I arrived to the meeting with Bob at 10 a.m. Fred started the meeting by calling roll for the people that should be in attendance. As I looked around, I found that many of the guys there were players who had previously said they weren't crossing—along with the ones who proclaimed as "on the fence." I didn't think anything of it as Fred called names and I waited for mine to come. I knew I was the last guy in camp, so I was expecting to be one of the last ones called, but Fred ended role without my name being called. That's when the doubt and fear started to set in.

Fred went on to speak for about 45 minutes and discussed all things that were pertinent with being on the road. These would include the dress policy, where to lease vehicles to get to and from the stadium, and other items we needed to know as the team that'd represent the Brewers at the start of the season. Fred went on to say there would be 39 players on the roster and 32 would go to Milwaukee to start the season. Of the 32 players, 25 would be considered "active" for each game, and this would vary each day. The starting pitchers would only be considered active once every four to five days for their start, this would leave nine relievers, seven bench players, and the nine starters for each game.

Most of the rest of what Fred talked about were details of acting on the road and understanding the privilege of the position we were in as a Major League baseball player. More than anything I was trying to cope with the problem I was having on why Fred didn't call my name. I had to believe that they had a number of pitchers decide to cross over the past couple of days. That would put me on the outside looking in. We had quite a few pitchers that pitched in games that spring, but not all of them said they'd pitch as a replacement player. I could only figure that they either were given an ultimatum, or they threw a bunch of money for them to sign.

Fred ended the meeting on a positive note from my perspective. He was told that the players' union would be contacting us again to keep us from crossing and management was 100% for the replacement players. If the strike were to find a settlement, then everybody in that room would be guaranteed a job in the organization once the players returned. These jobs would include going back to the minors, coaching, or scouting if that applied.

The thought of those words gave me hope because of the intention I had of wanting to stay involved in the game as a coach or a scout. Nevertheless, I was still having a hard time getting over the fact that my name wasn't called. I decided to talk with Sal Bando to see if he could shed light on the obvious omission during role.

"It must've been an error. I'm not sure why you're not on Fred's list. I apologize for that, and I'd understand why you'd feel this way, too—as if to believe that nobody knows you're around." Sal said with a concerning voice.

Sal advised me to go speak with Bill Castro and David Roe (ML pitching coach) to see how I was fitting into their plans, because they'd know more than he did. Later that day I caught up with Castro to see if he could let me know what was going on.

Bill let me know that I was slated to pitch in the minor league game against the Modesto A's (Oakland's A team) the next day, and I wouldn't be making the trip to the big league game. Castro didn't seem to be offering up any information that was helping me understand where I was fitting in.

"The competition is pretty tough," Bill said without any emotion.

"That's okay. The competition doesn't bother me. I think I've proven that point," I replied back to him.

"Why don't you go ask Sal what's going on?" Bill offered.

"I did speak with Sal. He told me to speak with you and Skid [Roe]," I said with a puzzled look.

Bill just shrugged his shoulders at that point and told me I was pitching in tomorrow's game against Modesto. I knew at that point I was overstepping my bounds by asking too many questions. I needed to just go to tomorrow's game and kick butt like I'd been doing at the major league level. It was really a test of how mentally tough I was going to have to be, but the way I was reacting to this was proving the opposite. This wouldn't be the first time I had felt slighted when it came to pitching, and feeling like I had performed well enough. The time I was pitching for Dick Prutting during that Saturday afternoon blowing away the entire team and never seeing the mound again was certainly coming to mind. *Why now? After all the good outings, why was I being demoted? And why couldn't any of the coaches come up to me and just tell me what was going on?*

I realized that I was getting ahead of myself and speculating on things that really hadn't been decided on at that point. Although I was slated to pitch in the minor league game, I didn't see the mound and went back in a big league game against the Angels a couple of days later. It was encouraging to know I was getting another chance with the big team and hoped to again prove my worth.

I was feeling great again in the bullpen before coming into the game in the ninth inning with the score tied 8-8. The Angels managed to bleed a couple of singles through the hole, and we ended up losing the game on a sacrifice fly ball 9-8. I was dejected as I walked off the mound with the runner scoring from third right in front of me.

Garner, Don Roe, and Billy all came up to me and told me I pitched well. They said that baseball can be that way sometimes—ground balls find holes even though you make a good pitch and get what you want. They also told me that each time I went out on the mound, my fastball had more velocity, and this game was the hardest I threw to date. The feeling was bittersweet after that. I wanted to hear all the good stuff they were saying, but I still lost, and that was the bottom line.

Here we were—now less than a week away—with 16 pitchers on the big league roster. It needed to be cut to 12. We found out that four pitchers from AAA accepted contracts to play as replacements. It really botched things up for my chances. Still, I hadn't been told to start practicing with any of the minor league clubs yet. Most of the team was set with only a few guys wondering where they were going to be—including myself. Other guys like Stacy Burdick, Scott Diez, Bobby, and a few others were on this bubble and feeling pretty much the same as me. The hardest thing to do was wait while the rest of your life would be affected in the next 24 to 48 hours when they finally set the rosters.

I spoke with one of the coaches about the frustration of waiting for the club to make their decision for the final rosters. Robbie Wine, one of the coaches who had been with the Brewers for a few years talked about the situation the previous year of Jeff Bronkey, a former minor league player.

"When are they going to say anything?" Jeff would say in earnest.

"If they don't say anything to you, you're going north with the team. You've done the best you can, and it's nothing that you can control." Robbie would say, trying to comfort Jeff's uneasiness.

It got to the point where Bronkey didn't hear anything from management, and was all ready to head to Milwaukee the day before the Brewers were scheduled to leave. He was called into their office and got word he was heading to AAA, New Orleans. It was that type of unknown that could drive players crazy.

Everybody wanted to know who was going to get left behind. They made their own lists of what they perceived as the depth charts and tried to figure out where they stood. The problem was that it was only their opinion. Nobody knew what the coaches and GM were thinking. It was something that players did in vain to try to cope with the eventuality of getting cut. One replacement pitcher was telling me that week that everybody in camp had been doing it for years.

"We've all got our lists made out, and we know who all the bubble guys are!" he said.

This was a week of reflection of how far we had come. The week moved so slow because of our fears of the unknown.

Baseball itself was actually moving very quickly as the season was approaching. On March 15, the MLBPA filed a grievance, and it took two weeks for the injunction to be expedited by the National Labor Relations Board (NLRB). The MLBPA informed the board that if the injunction was granted, they'd return to work and the teams would be subject to lawsuits if the players were locked out. Realizing the possibility of lawsuits, some of the teams backed down on voting for a lockout of the players and this was all the MLBPA needed.

If the injunction was granted, the players and owners would go back to the old agreement and continue playing until they had a new agreement. The problem for this was avoiding another strike by the players in the future. Another problem was would the players and owners bargain in good faith while the season was commencing? If the players didn't like how the negotiations were going, what would prevent them from striking again down the road?

During the last days of March, the talks progressed, and each day it seemed the situation changed. The final team going north still hadn't been announced and Phil wanted to have one last meeting with the players.

"Everything is status quo as far as we're concerned, and we're planning on being in Anaheim on Sunday for opening day," Garner said.

"The new proposal by the owners had one significant change in regards to salary arbitration and the players are considering it. Much is riding on the ruling for the injunction, so we'll have to see how things shake out in the next day or two," Phil concluded.

Because nearly all of the coaches on the Brewers were former players, many current players wanted to know what they thought of the new changes proposed by the owners. They all said that it looked good on the outside and needed to be considered, but it really needed to be looked at in depth. There was also talk of the owners wanting a "No-Strike" clause in case the injunction was granted to prevent a lockout. More than anything that meant all the lawyers had to give them the A-Okay before they signed it.

Another player asked Garner whether the team had been decided upon. It certainly was the "elephant" in the room. Many thought that it was the reason for the meeting in the first place.

Phil got up and addressed the question. "Guys, I apologize...the staff's still not sure on the final roster. We'll get back with you over the next few days," he said.

Well, there were about 10 players in the room (including myself) that his answer didn't sit well with. We all had an idea of what the final roster would be, but with all the talks of an injunction that'd effectively end the strike, why tell a bunch of players you're not going to Anaheim with us? Essentially by waiting, it gave them time to get them off the hook without hurting the guys that had helped them get through a very successful spring season for the Brewers. All of the players in camp were treated with respect, fairness, and like Major League ball players.

After the meeting, Brian Givens and I headed to the complex for batting practice before our game against the A's. I was on the list again to pitch and was excited to still be on the hunt for one of the last spots should the injunction fall through. We ended up winning the game 11-1 behind two home runs by Kenny Jackson, but I didn't get into the game. The game featured a couple of the guys who just crossed, and they needed to get innings to prepare for Anaheim. Don Roe came to me after the game and said I'd be going to the minor league game the next day and I should expect to pitch. It was the second time in as many trips that I was skipped, *and* told to go pitch in the minor league game the next day.

The next two nights were rough, trying to tell myself I had a chance to make it. Lying in bed I went over every mistake I made during my outings.

If I had only thrown this pitch instead—what was I thinking there?

The questions had no answers, and I'd just shake my head and try to deal with what was out of my control. Each night, I told myself I was thankful for just having the chance.

I'm willing to accept any fate that the Lord has in store for me.

With that, I turned out the lights and thought that tomorrow would be the first day for the rest of my life.

17 THE FIRST DAY OF THE REST OF MY LIFE

Going into my second minor league outing in a row, I thought it'd be a good time to explain the real side of professional baseball. Less than 10% of the players who signed a professional contract would get the chance to play one game in the show—but *every* player who signed one experiences minor league baseball. Major League players call it a rite of passage or paying your dues, but most all former professionals will call it "Hell" or "The Road to Nowhere."

Gone are the cameras, announcements of players, fans, and kids who want you to sign their baseball or hat before the games. Occasionally, you'd see some girlfriends of the players watching in the bleachers to support their baseball boyfriends, or in rare cases, husbands. Overall, it could be extraordinarily ordinary.

Starting for our team was a tall, right-handed pitcher with

an outstanding arm who was being groomed as a prospect in the organization. Judd had a fastball in the low 90s and pretty good control, but still was a novice in terms of understanding how to pitch effectively. Such was the case for a 20-year-old a couple of years out of high school. He would be slated in high A-ball Stockton and this would be his last start before the season would begin in California for him.

Judd didn't pitch too poorly on this day, giving up three runs in six innings of work. With that said, many of the opponents he faced hit the ball very hard off him, including a long home run. I came into the ninth inning and finished the game with the only blemish being that I hit a batter that was diving into the plate as I threw the ball on the inside part of it. Diving into the plate is something that a batter does to attack a pitched ball without any fear of getting hit by the pitch. Pitchers have to use their minds and pitch inside to make the hitter honest and respect that you are allowed to pitch inside, and they can't dive into the pitch without possibly getting hurt.

The manager of the Stockton Ports was Bob Mariano, and he had a team meeting after the game. Managers usually have a few words to say about the game, what was good and bad and what needs to be worked on for the next game. I was by far the oldest of the players there that day, and I decided to speak up about the issues our pitchers had regarding the protection of pitching inside to hitters.

"We had not pitched inside to these guys all game," I proclaimed. "Their hitters were diving into the plate, and we let them do this without the fear of getting hit. Look what happened when I went inside, he dove right into my fastball and got hit," I explained further. "We need to let the hitters we face know that we'll pitch inside and they could get hit if they try to dive into the pitch."

I wanted to let Mariano know that I understood baseball and how to pitch. I hoped that eventually I could coach and teach pitchers what I knew and had experienced, and that these things would prove valuable on this team or others. Bob thanked me for the input, and we all got ready for the bus ride back to Chandler.

I wasn't on the list to pitch in any games for the remainder of the week, and the replacement exhibition games were nearly over. Most all the players were now just waiting for the ruling on the injunction and if the owners had enough votes to lockout the players if it was granted. All in all, it looked as if the players were going to get what they wanted from the beginning. They liked playing under the current agreement, and it would revert back until they agreed on a new one. There would also be no guarantee that the players wouldn't go on strike again later that season.

It was said that neither side wanted this to be the way it would end and nobody expected there to be an agreement made in five months.

One player said, "It's like putting a Band-Aid over an open chest wound; it's not going to solve the problem."

Friday morning (March 30th) started out like any other day with us getting to Compadre Stadium, getting dressed to start up practice, and getting one of our last games in before packing up for Anaheim. Upon arriving at the clubhouse, I was told by the clubhouse attendant that Phil needed to see me after he was done speaking with someone in his office. With that, I turned to Bob, who was getting dressed at his locker.

"Bobby, that's it. Phil wants to see me. I'm going to be told that I'm not heading north to Milwaukee," I said, convinced.

"Ed, you don't know that. Stop guessing and see what he wants," Bobby said, not believing his own words.

As I walked into his office, Phil was with both Don Roe and Sal Bando and prepared to let me know my fate. I was very calm and prepared for the moment it came, as I had been thinking about what to say for when the day finally arrived.

"Ed, it's a numbers game. We're sending you back to minor league camp with the opportunity of being called up in case of an injury," Phil told me as I stood absorbing the news.

"Are there any other factors or criteria other than performance that were the deciding factors for the final roster?" I asked.

"When you get back to your assigned team, work on your timing," Phil said.

Sal interjected at this point, "You can collect your belongings, and somebody can help you get back to the minor league complex."

With that, they all shook my hand and thanked me for my hard work for the past six weeks at camp. And that was it. As I left Phil's office, the one last thing I said was about disagreeing with their decision.

"I understand why the decision was made," I told them. "Overall, I feel like I had a better spring than some of the other guys and deserved to make the squad. That being said, I can live with the decision because of all the reasons why I was here in the first place. I'll see you in about a month if we're still around."

I was surprised to feel like this weight had been lifted off my shoulders and I no longer had to worry about my fate. My suspicions were correct, even though I pitched better than many of the guys who were in the organization for years. I wouldn't get the chance to start in Milwaukee. I thought the decision was made in poor taste, but would I have made the same decision if I were in their shoes? Probably. The Brewers had thousands, perhaps hundreds of thousands of dollars invested in the players

I performed better than, while all they had invested in me was six weeks, a plane ticket, and a few thousand bucks. Scott Diez and Stacy Burdick were also sent to the minors; they were the guys that Phil, Don, and Sal were speaking with before me. Bobby Cuff was the only pitcher in camp that signed strictly as a replacement that made the club heading north. Every other pitcher in camp that made the squad had at least four years of pro experience.

Cleaning out my locker after the meeting was the hardest thing. Even though I was happy and I was no longer anxious about the deal, I had this feeling of failure while cleaning out my locker. I still felt like I had done my best and I could not have done anything differently. Pitching is not always about decision making. You make good decisions about the pitches you choose to throw, put them in good spots, and sometimes the hitter beats you. That's baseball. The non-playing decisions you make have much more impact when it comes to how far you make it in the pros.

Only the strike ending would've caused the demise of the replacement players who strictly signed on as such. My fate was still in my hands of eventually getting called up. Bobby was dealing with an incredible amount of pain due to the coaching staff using him on three days' rest over the past two weeks instead of four. He was happy that he'd be starting the season on the club, but was sure he couldn't last very long before being put on the DL. Of course, I was really happy for him—especially after all he went through this spring—but I figured he would be one of the guys that'd be the first to go. I told him I wouldn't be feeling sorry for him when he's freezing his ass off in Milwaukee and I was basking in the sunshine playing in El Paso!

The El Paso comment to Bobby was simply a way to try to soothe the stinging of getting sent down. The truth was, I'd love to be freezing in Milwaukee in a week or so, but that possibility wouldn't happen for a while. Scott and Stacy had gotten their things packed and had left for the minor league facility by this time. Bobby had dressed and was already at the game, so I was alone in the locker room as I took one last look and thought about the time playing here at Compadre Stadium.

One of the clubhouse attendants saw me walking toward the exit with my equipment bag and offered to give me a ride about a mile or so down the road to the complex. I told him thanks, but no, and went on my way. I needed the time to think about the times I had with the other players during the games, and the coaches who helped me improve as a pitcher. I also needed the time to transition into what I now was—a minor league player.

The first piece of business I needed to take care of was finding out if I was headed to New Orleans or El Paso. I figured it would be El Paso at the AA level because I had only been a professional for a couple of months. Speaking with Ed Durkin about what might happen should this occur was the same result because I was too old to be sent to Stockton. I also had a really good spring and had only given up two earned runs in my last seven appearances.

Fred was busy the entire morning due to all the changes being made and the associated paperwork. He finally let me in to see him, so I asked where I was going to be sent. I thought I was hearing things when he told me I was starting the season in Stockton.

I couldn't believe my ears—Stockton? Durkin said they wouldn't send me there. In the last 24 hours, I had essentially changed plans three times, and now I was going to Stockton and had no control over it. As I left Fred's office, I ran into Stacey and Scott, who were going to New Orleans and El Paso respectively, and given the day off from workouts.

"They are sending you to Stockton? You're kidding me!" Scott said in disbelief. "Fred told me I could have gone to Stockton, but he wouldn't do that to me...Stockton is brutal!"

Scotty and I just started laughing because it was senseless to do anything other than that. He quickly added, "Do you know that Stockton has one of the highest murder per capita rates in the United States?" he said laughing.

"Thanks for cheering me up, Flake," I said to Diez, using his nickname that had also been a moniker for other left-handed relief pitchers.

I found a locker to put my stuff in, thinking about what Scott said about Stockton. *Great...am I really going to go to a place that many people think is one of the armpits of the world? For $850 a month? Ugh...*I was told to dress out for the away game against Phoenix, the Cubs' single A team that afternoon, and would probably get some work out of the pen. I was a bit reluctant to go to the game, considering all the bad luck I'd had already. Would I be able to concentrate on the mound should they send me out there today? I decided to go in spite of my reservations.

I was 29 years old while most of these guys were 20 or 21. I felt more like their coach than their teammate. How was I going to fit in with these guys—let alone the fact I was a replacement player from the beginning? *Let's just get through this day and see what tomorrow has to bring. Time to get dressed and get on the bus to Phoenix for the game.*

I did get in and pitched the ninth inning, giving up a walk and a single, but not allowing a run to cross the plate. It was a typical inning for me in terms of the line score, but in my heart, I wasn't into it. If I was pitching in El Paso, I would've had more motivation, feeling like that was where I was supposed to end up. I went back to the hotel that night and gave Ed Durkin a call to let him know about what transpired today, and I got his feeling on what I should do.

Eddie always had a way to look at the bright side of things when it came to baseball. The eternal optimist was always positive, especially when it came to my situation. After all those years trying to get me signed and his boss Califano never signing off on me until the strike, Eddie was no different on the phone tonight.

"Eddie, you could be the guy from nowhere. Go to Stockton and let your ability to pitch get you promoted to a closer role or maybe even a starter. At least they didn't release you, which means they want you around!" Ed said with conviction.

Come to think of it, when it came to baseball, Ed always spoke his opinion with conviction. He was proud that I had performed well, and it certainly helped his position as a scout with the Brewers long after all this was over.

"Depending on what happens in Milwaukee, you can be sent there in a matter of weeks. Just a couple of breaks and you'll be up. Keep your head up." Durkin said.

Ed also added that this decision was probably monetarily driven. By sending me to Stockton, they would pay me less than half of what I would be payed if I went to El Paso or New Orleans. Another detail was the fact that this was my first professional contract and they wouldn't offer any more than that unless they tore it up and had me sign a new one for more money. It was no secret that the Brewers were cutting corners as much as possible when it came to expenses, and I was no different than any other expense. In the end, Ed had at least convinced me to stay for the moment.

After my conversation with Ed, I checked out what was going on with the injunction. The injunction was granted, and media sources were reporting that the scabs were not going to start the season. Peter Gammons of ESPN believed that the owners couldn't get the required 22 of 28 teams to vote "yes" on locking out the players. If that was truly the case, the season would be pushed back to late April or early May, and the season schedule would be modified. ESPN was also reporting that all the replacement players would be sent home.

With the granting of the injunction for the players, the only hope the replacements had at this point was the threat of a lockout by the owners because of the threat the players would just strike again before an agreement could be reached. The owners still hadn't officially voted to lock the players out, but they would have to make that decision before the first game in 36 hours. The timing couldn't be worse for the players in our position—the media was saying the owners were wary of possible lawsuits and who knows what else. I went to bed knowing the next day would be yet another news-filled day in camp and at the field. All the camps in Florida and Arizona would probably learn if these replacement players would play opening day.

18 REALITY IS STRANGER THAN...

I arrived at camp on Saturday morning, April Fools' Day, to learn that we were leaving for Stockton the next morning. Things had happened so fast; I hadn't even informed Lisa of what was going on. I felt guilty that I left her parents with the business while I was out here trying to be a part of baseball history, but to tell them I was planning on going to Stockton? I didn't even want to think about the ramifications of that conversation. They really would think I was just playing a joke on them because of what day it was.

Truth be told, I still wasn't completely sold on what I would do. I was leaning on going to California with the team to try to make a go of it, but something inside was asking why. If I left, there'd be no possible chance to get called up should a few guys get hurt, and that was a real possibility of happening. What would happen if I went to Stockton and just sat on the bench, knowing I was just there as an insurance policy for the big club?

As I got dressed for the game, I ran into four more pitchers that were signed yesterday as replacement players and would be with Stockton at the start of the season. These guys were players from other organizations in the cactus and grapefruit leagues that were let go, and Milwaukee had picked them up to start the season. I felt like I was back in competition all over again should some guys get injured in Milwaukee. I was starting to believe that I might not get the chance no matter what happened; they may bring one of these other guys up, or I might just get released, anyway. Do I stick it out and live with the consequences of the backlash of my family back home, or just ask for my release and say I gave it my best shot? Either way, I needed to make up my mind quickly because we were heading out the following day.

That afternoon, we were playing the Modesto A's and it was a scorching hot day without a cloud in the sky. Unlike Major League spring games, pitchers that weren't on the schedule to pitch still needed to show up to the game. I figured it would be a good time to chill and think about what decision I'd make about my future. Unlike the big league games that furnish bat and ball boys, these players needed to chase foul balls and pick up their own bats during the games. Just my luck, I was assigned to chase foul balls on the right field line for the entire game.

I was starting to think that the Lord was sending me a message from above. I'll tell you this; it was a really hot message, because I had to sit out in the bleachers with the sun beating down on me with no shade whatsoever. The minor league director, Fred Stanley, assigned certain spots for the designated ball boys to sit and they had no access to shade. Talk about adding insult to injury! Well, that was the life of a professional baseball player in a nutshell. Lou Holtz said it best when he quipped, "One day you're sipping the wine, the next day you're picking the grapes!"

Or in my case, chasing foul balls in Phoenix, Arizona...

It was during this time that I made the decision that I couldn't bear the thought of going to Stockton. It was rough enough to think about the sacrifice I'd be making monetarily, let alone dealing with Lisa and her parents if I went. I'd have to live in an apartment with some 21-year-old kid—something that didn't appeal to me, either. In short, this wasn't exactly a good hand to be dealt.

I went out there and played with some of the best players in the world; I held my own and had some real successes. I performed at every level of baseball in my career and had proven to myself that I was good. Whether you actually made the team or not was no longer important—ability and performance wouldn't always be the deciding factor to play on the big stage. Time after time during my baseball career this had been true. The people who said I wasn't good enough to play baseball at a high level were wrong, and I proved it over and over again. This was a battle that I knew I couldn't overcome. I was prepared to now to speak with Fred and talk about non-playing positions within the organization.

It was not a bad choice for me when thinking about being able to stay in the game. I figured I had the talent to work as a scout. I looked up to Durkin, and he could give me some pointers on how to be successful. Anyway, I figured I'd talk with him when we got back to Chandler.

Little did I know that the decision about my fate had already been decided. Fred addressed the Stockton team as a group when we arrived back in Chandler and told us the owners were not voting to lock the players out, effectively ending the strike.

"There will be some players on this team that won't be making the trip to Stockton tomorrow because the trickledown effect of the Major League players will affect all the lower classes," Fred said to the players, who listened intently.

"We have thirty-two replacement players that we have promised positions within the organization, and fifteen more players from the forty-man roster will be added to the minor leagues in about three weeks. That means we have almost fifty players that we need to reassign to five ball clubs and extended spring training," Fred concluded.

I knew right away that the organization was not sending me anywhere, let alone Stockton. They had promised me a place in the organization, but I had the feeling that it would be something I couldn't afford to take. I was almost certain one of the first things that Fred was going to do was address my situation, which included my release.

After the meeting was completed, my new pitching coach, Mark Littell, called me over. You may remember, he was the pitcher who gave up one of the most memorable home runs in MLB history. He was on the mound for the Kansas City Royals when Chris Chambliss of the New York Yankees hit the series winning home run to win the 1976 ALCS. The crowd stormed the field when it left the yard and the images of him trying to run the bases were legendary. They made Chambliss re-run the bases later because it was determined that nobody was sure if he actually touched them all in the fracas!

Anyway, Mark told me that Fred wanted to see me in his office.

"Thanks Mark, I already know he wants to see me. Thanks for helping me the last couple of days," I replied.

"How do you know that he wants to see you? When you're in there, send those guys back out here; they need to get their running in," he replied back.

I just smiled and thanked him again.

"Good luck this year in Stockton, Mark," I said as I left to go see Fred.

When I got back into the facility, I ran into one of the pitchers I had gotten acquainted with in my brief time with Stockton, Matt Murphy. Murph was one of those players with a dream of making the show and continued to have setbacks. He was in his third year with the Brewers and getting frustrated with Stanley because he wouldn't trade or release him. He'd been in Beloit for the past two years and had had a great season before he blew out his arm a year before. Now, he was at Stockton and hoping to give it just one last shot before calling it quits.

"Murph, Littell wants you guys to head back out to the field and get your running in," I said.

"Well, aren't you coming to run with us?" Matt said looking straight down at me while I was unlacing my spikes for the last time.

"No, I'm not going to be with you guys this year," I told him without looking up.

Matt replied back angrily, "You're still part of this team..."

I cut him off mid-sentence, "Listen, don't you understand? The strike is over, and the players aren't going to be locked out. I'm finished! I'm probably only going to be a professional for about another ten minutes!" I said with obvious disgust.

Matt just gave me a dismal look and headed out to run with the other pitchers. I don't think he really understood my position on the club—kind of like when Givey found out I was a replacement player earlier in the spring. Matt was just a kid, so I didn't really expect him to understand, anyway. I started down the facility hallway and entered Fred's office for the first and last time of my life.

"Ed, when you were sent to Stockton yesterday, you became part of the minor league Brewer organization. Once you were no longer a part of the replacement team, the guarantee of employment no longer applied," Fred said.

I hadn't thought that out as of yet. I knew I'd signed a minor league contract with Durkin, but I was unaware that my role as a replacement player had ceased when I was sent down. Basically, I was a minor league pitcher that was considered too old to keep on one of the lower levels and take innings away from other pitchers in the organization. This wasn't really an issue with me because I knew I wouldn't be offered a playing position with the club.

Fred continued, "Because of the situation, I can't keep you in Stockton."

"I already know that, Fred. I was aware of that," I said matter-of-factly.

"I can't offer you a position in Beloit, and I don't have enough positions here at Chandler for extended spring training," Fred continued as he looked at me for reaction to his words.

"I already know that too, Fred. I knew that before you told Mark to send me in here," I said.

"Ed, I know some managers in the Texas-Louisiana Independent League that I can get you a contract with if you're interested," he said offering a suggestive head nod to me.

"Fred, I'm not interested in taking a roster spot from some kid that has the possibility of making it, because in the eyes of professional baseball, I'm not a prospect," I continued. "I'm also not so selfish to take that spot from somebody who has a chance. I'd just like a recommendation from you and Sal to the head of the scouting department to give me a shot in that direction."

Fred agreed to have that done, and I left his office feeling satisfied that I'd accomplished what I had set out to do. I got back in the clubhouse when many of the same guys I was with on the Stockton roster were finding out they were going to different clubs, including Matt.

"I can't go back to Beloit," he said in a disheartened fashion. "I already asked Stanley for a trade, but he won't trade me. I asked for my release, and he refused to do that too, telling me, 'So you can go to some other team and do well?' This game sucks..."

As I was collecting my belongings for the second time in as many days, many of the Stockton players couldn't believe that I got released. I told them that my purpose for being there had been completed and my services were no longer needed.

Another player stopped me and said, "What's the difference? Everybody knows you can pitch. Why are you letting them do this to you? Why don't you fight for getting your job back because you're good enough to pitch here?"

"I understand why you'd feel that way. I came here to play and prove I could compete with the other players on this team and the other teams this spring. I did that. Now, it's time to move on and get on with the rest of my life. Respect from players such as yourselves means more to me than fighting for a job that belongs to one of you," I said.

I left the facility for the last time and wished the players well that year. I wanted to get back to the hotel and talk with Bobby and the rest of the guys to see what had happened with them. I knew Scott and Stacy had the same fate as me, but Bob was on the replacement team and was guaranteed a position in the organization. It'd be interesting to see if he took it. At his age, he'd have to go to El Paso as Ed Durkin had said.

When I arrived at the hotel, I saw that a bunch of the guys were outside their rooms talking, including Bobby. What I didn't expect over the next few minutes was a conversation that was not only unexpected—but hard to accept, too.

Sometimes the things you do as a person can have all the right intentions, yet the opposite effect. Over the years, I have learned that in arguments I've had with relatives, friends, my now ex-wife, and my children. Every argument I've had, I always learned from it, trying to take something positive from a negative situation. This time, it was going to be a big one.

Over my time in Arizona, I'd been a bit outspoken, to say the least. It'd been my nature to speak the truth about right and wrong. I had dealt with the media and coaches about things that were implied and things that were said, and every time, I stood up for myself without any malicious intentions. Things were about to change.

The talk around the beer cooler that evening was how I had "showed up" a pitcher earlier that week, and during the couple of hours before I got there, players were talking openly about it. All of them knew that Bob and I were tight and apparently they were giving him a lot of grief for what I had done. When I walked into the bear trap disguised as players drinking beer outside the hotel room, Bobby decided to let me know about it.

He went on to explain, in front of about six other players, how I showed up Judd Wilstead in front of the entire Stockton team. He went on to say how I embarrassed Judd by explaining how he didn't establish the inside part of the plate and that's why some of the hitters teed off on him. Then, with the help of a few Budweisers, Bob explained how I ought to think more often before I open my mouth and continued to show me up in front of the team. He just went on and on as I tried to step in and defend myself, but there was no use in this situation. Anything I said at this point would've been useless, but I tried to defend my actions. I told Bob and the others that I had no malicious intent on showing up anybody. It was the coach coming out in me. I was making an observation on the game and spoke my mind. As

I left to go back to my room, I told him that what he just did to me was just as bad—if not worse. Deliberately saying those things in front of everybody was in much poorer taste than what I'd done the other day, and maybe he should look in the mirror before accusing somebody of showing a teammate up.

Things only escalated afterward when I confronted Bobby later on as I told him again I had no intention of showing Wilstead up. I decided to write Judd a letter that I had become aware of what was perceived as a mistake. I knew my time in Arizona had come to an end and the last thing I wanted to do was be around a bunch of players who had talked about my apparent gaffe. I found myself packing my things in my room and called for a taxi to get me to the airport. I headed back to Florida for good.

The time immediately after the owners gave up locking out the players was obviously that of great joy to the media. They were satisfied with the results and proclaimed how it would have been a "travesty" if Marty Clary had thrown that first pitch for the Marlins in the first replacement game on opening day. The MLBPA had the players out there doing interviews for damage control to appeal to the group of people that most wanted to see us play for at least one game—the fans.

Many of them talked about how it was a relief to provide for their families again and be able to put food on the table. It was hard to listen at times, as if we talked about a factory worker in Pennsylvania who lost his job because of mechanical automation and a robot now has his job. What about the auto makers in Detroit who went on strike to get better benefits for their families? Do you think they related to these players when they talked about being able to put food on the table? I think not.

Lenny Dykstra from the Phillies came on Roy Firestone's "Up Close" on ESPN and told Roy how they (MLB players) needed to do more for the fans. "It's the fans that are getting (explicative) screwed!" he told a media source in his interview. "We have to show them more than we have lately," Dykstra finished his rant.

Thanks Lenny, for that vital piece of information. Would you still feel that way when you and the rest of the MLBPA were talking strike again in August later in the year?

Brady Anderson of the Baltimore Orioles was also on the "Up Close" Firestone piece and was confronted by Roy with the question, "If there is no agreement by August, would you go back on strike?"

Anderson replied, "If we had to, yes, but nobody wants a strike."

Anderson's statement was perhaps the most telling. His indication that the MLBPA would go back on strike was that they virtually learned nothing from the past eight months. From the players' point of view, there were some that genuinely believed the fans were the biggest losers and said all the right things—but after all this, could we believe this? Right now, I think they were all breathing a sigh of relief and time would heal the wounds that the players and the owners had created for themselves.

The experiences I had while playing during the replacement exhibition games gave me the perspective that not all the fans wanted to see the striking players back so soon. Speaking with many of the fans during those games, they had nothing but support. They enjoyed the games as if it were any other spring in Arizona. The guys on the field hustled and played with passion and enjoyment. They connected with those that came out to see them play in those six weeks before the strike ended. With the players before the strike, there was something missing. Some say it was just the way players communicated with the people who watched them play. There was this feeling of entitlement that had permeated the minds of the players that we should feel privileged to watch them play and be in their space. For the most part, back in the day of the fifties and sixties, if somebody wanted an autograph, the player might blush and feel honored to sign a ball or two—now it's just an annoying part of the game.

Tony LaRussa, the coach of the Chicago White Sox, put it best after the players came back. "I should tell my players to watch these guys playing to let them understand what this game is all about."

For now, the players would be on their best behavior, doing what they could to repair the damage of their greed and misuse of the hands that fed them. The owners played a huge part in this ordeal as well, not understanding how to effectively run their organizations without taking the toll on the fans from the financial ramifications of free agency and salary caps. Overall, it would be hard to imagine if both sides will ever be in harmony when it comes to splitting billions of dollars.

Now that I'd turned back to being a spectator and an amateur baseball player, I was finding it difficult to want to root for my favorite team, the Yankees. Through all of this, I have lost respect for how they treated the people and players in their own organizations. The way Surhoff spoke to the minor league players in the meetings leading up to the first exhibition game gave me a new perspective of how this game had changed. Unfortunately, it wouldn't be too long until it was back to the way it was and all the parties involved wouldn't acknowledge that this strike ever happened.

The value that this country has placed on baseball and other professional sports is too high to be treated with such disrespect by those participants who are directly involved in the sport. Baseball is a game so loved and endeared by millions, played by children and amateur adults, and professionally by only a few thousand, but the basics are the same. Maybe a professional star could come out and appease the players to signal out to the fans of the world, and give us the respect we were owed. Was that really a far-fetched idea for the 1990s? Someone must stand up and let us know we were appreciated—and let them know the game they play so well is OURS, not theirs. Always remember, without us, there was no game; there were no television contracts, no appearance fees—no nothing. A little voice inside my heart had told me not to hold my breath, and I knew I was always going to have more fun coaching and playing the game than watching it.

EPILOGUE

Shortly after getting back to Tampa, our lives that had been interrupted for the past three months started to get back to normal. Bobby went back to the VA and I went back to the family business and our season with the Hurricanes had already gotten underway without us. As much as we wanted to play at least one regular season game with the Brewers, our mission was still a success to us. We played and played well against the seasoned AA and AAA veterans that had been there for many years. More than anything, it brought us closure and we could move on from professional baseball.

Bobby and I talked about the evening in Arizona after the strike had ended and decided it was a difficult day for both of us. We both regretted some things and decided to move on and not let it affect our friendship. Looking back on that evening I am happy we could put it behind us. I am truly grateful that we are good friends to this day and I very much value his friendship.

One of the things Bobby and I would do on a regular basis was get together on Tuesday nights and play sports trivia at one of the local restaurants in Clearwater. Occasionally there was another guy Eric who showed up there regularly and asked why we hadn't been there in so long. Bobby and I told him that we had just gotten back from Arizona where we were replacement players for Milwaukee.

Eric was excited to hear about our experience and told us he was friends with one of the producers at Channel 10 news in Tampa. He asked us if we would like to go on the air and talk a little about our experience in Arizona because the people would be interested in hearing what we had to say. I was surprised to hear Bobby decline the invitation; he had told me that working at the VA had influenced his decision and didn't want to go public. I told Eric I would love to talk about it and shortly after, I received a phone call from the station.

The producer told me that a reporter would come to my home and interview me there and it would be a five-minute segment. Late that afternoon the news team arrived and the reporter, much to my surprise, was the beautiful Lisa Foronda. As she and the cameraman were walking up to the door, all I could think about was being able to get through the interview!

After a few minutes of getting the microphone on and doing some test checks they were ready for the interview. As far as the questions that Foronda asked, they were mostly generic. What was it like? How did the people respond? Did the coaches treat you differently...etc., etc. My responses were all positive and I told them how grateful I was to the Milwaukee Brewers organization for allowing me the opportunity to play during spring training.

The segment ended as I told them of all the notes I took during the time I was there in preparation for writing this book. The camera panned on all the handwritten pages of notes, including the one with the title *Scabs Heal All Wounds.* In a way, I had now obligated myself to complete the task of writing this book.

Later that evening on the 11:00 o'clock news, the segment that was shot earlier that day was shown. They had interviewed another player that signed as a replacement player with the Blue Jays and interviewed him as well for the segment. It was a contrasting viewpoint as my interview was the positive side and his the negative.

The player went on and told the reporter about how they were used by the team and made false promises and just jettisoned us the day after the strike ended. He was clearly bitter that the Blue Jays didn't keep him in the organization and wanted to let the public know about it. The only thought that came across my mind as I watched him talk was, *What did you think they were going to do?*

The players and owners eventually signed a new CBA and MLB has gone over 20 seasons without a work stoppage. In December of 2016, there were grumblings of yet another work stoppage with new topics for discussion and how to handle them moving forward. The increase of international players since 1995 has been nothing short of spectacular. The increase of Cuban players defecting to come to the U.S. and play baseball created much tension between the two countries as well as how to handle who has the rights for those players' services. Players born in the U.S. have to go through the draft...these players coming out of Cuba are given multi-million dollar contracts as if they were unrestricted free agents. The talks about an International Draft were discussed for future CBAs to deal with this problem.

I only mention this to discuss the overall changes that MLB has seen in the past 20 years since the work stoppage in 1995. Did the strike in 1995 make the game better? Has the game improved in comparison to the other professional sports in the U.S., or have they lost market share? Has MLB built their brand to withstand the changes in demographics, viewership, fan base and marketplace? Lastly, what can we expect over the next 25 years and where will baseball most likely be in terms of that phrase "America's Pastime"...?

It was evident that MLB took a major hit after the strike as many die-hard baseball fans vowed never to watch the game again. Some of them kept their word but many eventually came back to the game they enjoyed watching since their childhood. Then, in 1998, came the home run battle between two of the most colorful players in the game—Mark McGuire and Sammy Sosa. Both players were on pace to break the single season home run record set by Roger Maris in 1961. Many people, including most of the media, gave those two players the credit for saving major league baseball from the massive negativity left in the wake of 1995. By the end of the season McGuire blasted 70 home runs and destroyed the old record of 61 by an amazing 15%. Sosa also surpassed Maris that year with 66 homers—an astounding accomplishment as well. What we didn't know was that an ugly backdrop was about to reveal itself and create more controversy about that season, the use of performance enhancing drugs (PEDs).

For many decades players would try many things to help get them through the rigors of a 154 or 162 game season. Many players in the past have admitted to using amphetamines or "greenies" as they were called in the industry. Greenies would help keep them from getting tired after many stretches of playing a 9-inning game for 10-15 days in a row. Nobody thought of them as a PED, but in retrospect, it played a part in helping improve how a player performed on the field that day. In my mind, it didn't really make you a better player, it only kept you from being tired for short periods of time. Steroids are completely different.

Steroids artificially create more muscle, and make injuries heal faster than without them. Players have made claims that it helps improve their eyesight, arguably the most important sense a baseball player needs. More muscle lead to greater bat speed. Baseballs that were once hit close to the fence are now going over it. This impacted the game and artificially boosted statistics that would impact the players' salaries from 1997 to the present day. Pitchers saw the impact of how players like McGuire, Sosa, Barry Bonds, Rafael Palmeiro, and Alex Rodriguez had on the baseball field and decided they needed to take them as well. There had been reports that nearly 90% of all MLB players were on some form of PED during the late '90s and through early 2000s. One MLB player from the early to middle 2000s told me that his personal estimation of PED use in MLB was over 80%.

The issue of steroids in baseball was not only on the field of play but off. The effect on the overall financial results to salary negotiations, advertising, ticket prices, and television rights was much more impactful.

As ticket prices started to soar, many people on fixed incomes in smaller markets like Tampa, Kansas City, and Minneapolis stopped going to baseball games. As attendance dropped, broadcast ratings rose. The increased ratings created more demand by the owners to have advertisers pay higher premiums to cover their team in the local market. This was also happening with the large market teams.

Television networks like YES (NY Yankees), NESN (Red Sox), WGN (Cubs), TBS (Braves) had also seen increases in ratings for their teams as well while ticket sales remained static. Hence, over the past 20 years with the advent of large screen HDTVs combined with the soaring ticket and concession prices, people have decided to attend fewer games—plain and simple.

Over the past few years, television ratings started to drop across the board with the few exceptions of those teams in contention for the World Series. The average age of baseball viewers for the World Series in 2004 was 46 and increased to 53 in 2014 according to the *Washington Post*. Inversely, the number of viewers for the World Series has decreased from over 25 million in 2004 to about 12 million in 2014. These are numbers that have continued to trend downward with no end in sight. Can MLB continue to exist today with this downward spiraling popularity and survive? Let's look at some of the numbers...

Since 1980, players' salaries have increased at a rate eight times faster in comparison to the average worker in the U.S. The average salary in the U.S. in 1980 was $12,517 and the average salary for a player in MLB was $143,676. Today, the average salary in the U.S. is $44,569—or 3.5 times what the average worker made in 1980. In MLB, the average salary in 2015 was $3,952,252—a whopping 27.5 times what they made in 1980! For comparison, the average NFL salaries in 1980 and 2015 were about half that of MLB.

Player negotiations with general managers and owners haven't changed over the years, but the rights for television broadcasts through the various networks have. With all the new-found money in the television rights, owners started giving more money to the players as they constantly tried to outbid the others for the signing of free agents. The MLBPA is in its glory! The MLBPA has an unwritten rule regarding negotiations—the player always takes the highest offer, even if the player would rather take less and play somewhere else. This will virtually guarantee that the salary pool will go up and in turn the owners would pass the expense to the advertisers. Owners know that players' salaries are paid mostly by the television deals made with the networks. Advertisers will continue to pay if the ratings stay high. However, when the time comes that the cost exceeds the ratings, those advertisers will pull out and renegotiate the deals.

When I was growing up, going to a Yankees or Mets game was a wonderful experience. Going to those games as a teenager was one of the main reasons why I fell in love with the sport and decided to pursue my dreams of playing in college and eventually as a pro. Today, there is less interest by the younger generation to be involved in baseball. According to the salary figures I just spoke of, it is evident that parents have less disposable income than ever before, while prices to attend games have risen at much higher rates than inflation over the past 30 years. The NFL, NBA, and newer sports like MMA (Mixed Martial Arts) are more interesting to America's youth. Twenty years from now, we will have lost an entire generation due to the lack of interest of today's youth. The latest poll conducted by Harris Research supports this supposition.

In 1985, the Harris Research Poll conducted a survey of the most popular sports in the United States and the NFL edged out MLB 24% to 23%. In 2014, those numbers changed drastically, with the NFL at 35% to just 14% for MLB. It is estimated that MLB will fall out of the top five sports in this country by the year 2035...why such the rapid decline in popularity? It is certain that there is a lack of interest by our youth when you add the fact that the average age of baseball viewers is increasing every year.

I bring this to attention because I feel this sport is at a crossroads in this country. I would have never believed it would be possible that baseball in the United States would lose its popularity as much as it already has. All research points to this trend continuing for decades to come unless the owners, players' union and its partners correct the issues with the current generation in this country.

To baseball's credit, they have taken some proactive steps to make the game more palatable to the restless viewer. Speeding up time between innings and elimination of thrown pitches in the intentional walk are good starts, but hardly a way to bring in new viewers. I just don't believe there are many other ways to speed up a baseball game! The way a baseball game is played out is just its very nature—it's not designed to be constant motion and movement. It shouldn't be any other way either. For me, some of the most tense and enjoyable moments in a baseball game are the times before the pitcher throws the ball and nobody on the field is moving.

Despite what the "old-school" baseball fan believes makes the game interesting, that doesn't mean the current generation will think so. You cannot make the game what it's not, so as of now, this country will see baseball fade away into the rearview mirror. Think about how the game became popular in the first place... For decades, the fathers in this country have taken their kids to ballgames and started the tradition. The millennial generation that has nearly zero interest will not be carrying on that tradition. They will be at home with their kids bonding over sports like MMA and the NFL, which are designed to be watched at home. There may be the occasional grandparent who still would like to take the kids to a baseball game, but the excitement is not nearly what it once was. This may add a few fans, but not enough to overcome the previous 30 years of disinterest. In other words, MLB is terminally ill and although it won't go extinct, it will never be like it is today.

There are some glimmers of hope, but they don't rest with us—they rest with those countries outside the U.S. Baseball is growing internationally at a much greater rate than it is here. This year's World's Baseball Classic (WBC) was a rousing success and all expectations are that this will continue. Every club, besides Cuba, was represented in the tournament and had players that were in MLB or their minor-league affiliates. As the interest grows in the world maybe the natural direction of MLB is growing a yearly world competition. A league is formed combining the professional leagues around the world and culminates in a literal "World Series." As popularity grows worldwide, new revenue streams enter and players can possibly make up for the lack of interest stateside. Then there is the hope that generations to come recreate the desire to watch the game as we did decades before, only this time on a world stage.

Another way to save the sport in this country is to have a concerted grassroots effort by MLB itself. Each area that a MLB team considers its base should work in consortium with local leadership in developing baseball for the early ages of our youth. Each owner has a vested interest in keeping our future generations interested in the sport and at this moment, participation in youth baseball compared to other sports is declining.

One of the ways to increase interest is to facilitate change and bring kids back to the sport. I'm not speaking of kids who are already interested in the game, I'm talking about the kids who think the game is boring and doesn't have the same action of other sports. If ML teams can sponsor leagues and have the players and managers volunteer their time to bring kids out to play, it could change the ideology that baseball is not only "cool," but fun to play. They, in turn, may have a different view of the game and pass that to the next generation, like my father did for me. This is not happening with our current generation and baseball will suffer. Acting now may be the only chance they have for the next generation of kids in the future.

I know these ideas are general; I can only hope to see some of the shift before I become part of the past. It's time for a new kind of CBA to happen in MLB. I would call it a "CBA between the owners/players and the fans who support the game." The owners and players can let the fans know what they're going to do to help the game grow again. Make it more affordable for the average fan, invest in our community youth baseball programs, and volunteer your time with the kids. Now is the time...

REFERENCE MATERIAL

1. **"1994-1995 Baseball Strike"** *Wikipedia* **14 Feb 2017 3 March 2017** https://en.wikipedia.org/wiki/1994%E2%80%9395_Major_League_Baseball_strike

2. **Definition "Scab"** *Dictionary.com* **23 April 2017** http://www.dictionary.com/browse/scab?s=t

3. **Rose, Charlie "Bob Costas talks about the baseball strike"** *Charlie Rose* **14 Sept 1994** https://charlierose.com/videos/22145

4. **Chadwick ID 0ca6a3bf "Tim Dell"** *Baseball Refence.com* **23 April 2017** http://www.baseball-reference.com/register/player.fcgi?id=dell--001tim

5. **"Major League anti-trust reform"** *A bill to require the general application of the anti-trust laws to Major League Baseball, and for other purposes"* **17 June 1997 Committee on the judiciary United States Senate 17 June 1997** https://archive.org/stream/MajorLeagueBaseballAntitrustReform/SJud061797_djvu.txt

6. **"Probability of playing college and professional baseball"** *The High School Baseball Web"* **26 April 2017** http://www.hsbaseballweb.com/probability.htm

7. **"Gayle Sierens"** *Wikipedia* **24 Feb 2017 23 April 2017** https://en.wikipedia.org/wiki/Gayle_Sierens

8. **"Deion Sanders Top Moments"** *Wilson Report Seminoles.com* **6 August 2009 23 April 2017** http://www.seminoles.com/ViewArticle.dbml?DB_OEM_ID=32900&ATCLID=209543859

9. **Haudricourt, Tom "Barker finds replacement decision tough" Milwaukee Journal Sentinel 14 March 1995 23 April 2017** http://nl.newsbank.com/nl-

search/we/Archives?p_multi=MWSB|PKPB&p_product=
MSNP&p_theme=msnp&p_action=search&p_maxdocs=
200&s_dispstring=%20Tim%20Barker%20AND%20date(1
995)&p_field_date-0=YMD_date&p_params_date-
0=date:B,E&p_text_date-0=1995&p_field_advanced-
0=&p_text_advanced-
0=(%20Tim%20Barker)&xcal_numdocs=20&p_perpage=
10&p_sort=_rank_:D&xcal_ranksort=4&xcal_useweights
=yes

10. "Brian Givens" *Baseball Reference.com* 23 April 2017
http://www.baseball-
reference.com/players/g/givenbr01.shtml

11. "Brian Givens" *Wikipedia* 17 December 2016 23 April
2017 https://en.wikipedia.org/wiki/Brian_Givens

12. "Bill Dobrolsky" *Baseball Reference.com* 23 April 2017
http://www.baseball-
reference.com/register/player.fcgi?id=dobrol001wil

13. Fisher, Marc "Baseball is struggling to hook kids—and
risks losing fans to other sports" *The Washington Post* 5
April 2015 23 April 2017
https://www.washingtonpost.com/sports/nationals/bas
eballs-trouble-with-the-youth-curve--and-what-that-
means-for-the-game/2015/04/05/2da36dca-d7e8-11e4-
8103-
fa84725dbf9d_story.html?utm_term=.d447a230dd00

14. Shaiken, Bill "A look at how Major League Baseball
salaries have grown more than 20,000% the last 50
years" *Los Angeles Times* 28 March 2016 23 April 2017
http://www.latimes.com/sports/mlb/la-sp-mlb-salaries-
chart-20160329-story.html

15. "National Average Wage Index" *Social Security
Administration* 23 April 2017
https://www.ssa.gov/OACT/COLA/AWI.html

16. **Shannon-Missal, Larry "Pro Football is still America's favorite sport"** *The Harris Poll* **26 Jan 2016 23 April 2017** http://www.theharrispoll.com/sports/Americas_Fav_Sp ort_2016.html

ABOUT THE AUTHOR

Photograph by Matthew Bilancia at Lux Pictures

Edward Porcelli was born and raised in Fairfield County, Connecticut and moved to Tampa, Florida in the summer of 1983. He graduated from Florida State University with a BA in Literature in May of 1988.

Ed has been an entrepreneur since graduating from FSU. He currently works as a commercial real estate agent in Tampa for FHR Commercial, LLC.

Ed also continued playing baseball in amateur leagues until he retired at age 50 in 2015. He now stays involved in the sport as the pitching coach for the Pasco-Hernando State

Conquistadors in New Port Richey, Florida. He and his wife Suzanne relocated to Chapel Hill, North Carolina in the summer of 2017.

Ed has also co-written a screenplay with Shawn Powell of SPI in Tampa about the 1995 MLB strike, titled *30 Pieces Of Silver*, and is currently marketing it to various production companies.

On the home front, Ed enjoys spending time with his wife and their three daughters—Kristin, Kaitlyn, and Jennifer.

Made in the USA
Columbia, SC
16 September 2021